Religion,
Homosexuality and Literature

Gay Men's Issues in Religious Studies Series,
Volume 3

Proceedings of the Gay Men's Issues in Religion Group
of the American Academy of Religion,
Fall 1990

Edited by

Michael L. Stemmeler
&
José Ignacio Cabezón

Las Colinas
Monument Press
1992

Published by
Monument Press
Las Colinas, Texas

This is Volume 3 in the Gay Men's Issues in Religious Studies, Proceedings of the Gay Men's Issues in Religion Consultation of the American Academy of Religion.

Library of Congress Cataloging-in-Publication Data

Religion, homosexuality, and literature / essays by Gary David Comstock ... [et al.] ; with an introduction by Josè Ignacio Cabezòn ; edited by Michael L. Stemmeler & J. Michael Clark.
p. cm. -- (Gay men's issues in religious studies series ; v. 3)
Chiefly papers presented in the Gay Men's Issues in Religious Group program of the American Academy of Religion meeting held in New Orleans, La., fall 1990.
Includes translation of: Shin'yuk i.
Includes bibliographical references.
ISBN 0-930383-28-1 (pbk.) : $10.00 ($12.00 Can.)
1. Homosexuality--Religious aspects--Congresses. 2. Gay men--Religious life--History--Congresses. 3. Homosexuality in literature--Congresses. 4. Religious literature--Congresses.
I. Comstock, Gary David, 1945- . II. American Academy of Religion. Gay Men's Issues in Religion Group. III. Shin'yuk i, English, 1992. IV. Series.
BL65.H64R45 1992
291.1'78357662--dc20 92-24252
CIP

— III —

Gay Men's Issues in Religious Studies Series

under the general editorship of

J. Michael Clark & Michael L. Stemmeler

Forthcoming

in the

***Gay. Men's Issues
in
Religious Studies Series:***

Volume 4

Proceedings of the Gay Men's Issues
in Religion Group, American Academy of Religion
Fall 1991, Kansas City

Gay Affirmative Ethics

including papers by
J. Michael Clark,
Jeffrey Hopkins,
Yoel Kahn,
Bob McNeir,
Craig W. Pilant, &
Michael L. Stemmeler,
with a response by
Mark R. Kowalewski

* * *

Table of Contents

I. **Preface**
- Michael L. Stemmeler 1

II. **Introduction: Religion, Homosexuality and Literature**
- José Ignacio Cabezón 3

III. **Love, Power and Competition Among Men in Hebrew Scripture: Jonathan as Unconventional Nurturer**
- Gary David Comstock 9

IV. **Ramakrishna's Foot: Mystical Homoeroticism in the Kathāmṛta**
- Jeffrey J. Kripal 31

V. **Spiritual Dimensions of Male Beauty in Japanese Buddhism**
- Paul Gordon Schalow 75

VI. **Taoist Themes in Chinese Homoerotic Tales**
- Giovanni Vitiello 95

VII. **Notes on Contributors** 105

I. Michael L. Stemmeler

Preface

The contributors to the third volume in the *Gay Men's Issues in Religious Studies Series* are happy to present you their work. It reflects the result of the Gay Men's Issues in Religion Group's program unit at the 1990 meeting of the American Academy of Religion in New Orleans, LA. In addition to the papers read in New Orleans, this volume includes Jeffrey J. Kripal's paper *Ramakrishna's Foot*. The introduction by José Ignacio Cabezón comments upon all four essays.

It is my sincere hope that the scholarship presented in this collection finds your undivided approval. As was the case with volumes 1 and 2 of this series, a variety of contributors is again involved in this project. The range spans from graduate student to established scholar of religious studies. Each one of them has produced an outstanding piece of work and is eager to offer his contribution to the scholarly world. Thematically, this volume addresses numerous issues in the interrelationship of religion, homosexuality and literature. The essays guide the reader from an investigation of the Hebrew Scriptures (love and power) to a study of Hindu and Buddhist literature (mysticism and spirituality), followed by an analysis of Chinese tales with Taoist themes (homoeroticism).

Thanks go to the authors for focusing their and the reader's attention on a seldom visited field of scholarship. Your patience and diligence in reading these essays is greatly appreciated. I am sure the reward will be yours in the end.

Mt. Pleasant, Michigan
10 April 1992
National Day of Action
for Lesbian, Gay and Bisexual Rights

II. José Ignacio Cabezón

Introduction: Religion, Homosexuality and Literature

The fact of the love between men, that is, its mere existence, may be a transhistorical and cross-cultural universal, since male homosexual love is to be found in most societies and in almost all periods of human history for which we have documentation; but the *nature* and *character* of this love is an historically and culturally conditioned phenomenon. In some places and times homosexual love, even when it has been expressed in fully sexual ways, has found social acceptance. In other periods of human history even the fraternal and filial expression of male love, not to speak of its expression in sexual ways, has been socially proscribed. This diversity in social attitudes toward male love[1] has been reflected in the world's religious and secular literature, though the relationship of social attitudes to the literary depiction of male love is by no means a linear and straightforward one. Social intolerance of homosexuality has not prevented literati from depicting—even from sympathetically portraying—male love, even in religious texts that otherwise portray homosexuality in a generally negative light. In societies where there have been no religious obstacles to male love, as might be expected, we find the full range of human symbols—including religious ones—used to interpret and to extol the love between men, or between men and boys. Although the essays in this volume deal with radically different cultures and periods in human history—ancient Israel, nineteenth century Hinduism, classical China and premodern Japan—they are all preoccupied with a number of common themes: male love, its depiction in literature, the degree of social acceptability it enjoys (if any) in a given culture, and the relationship of religion to each of the above.

Now the four essays in this volume explore different questions by variously emphasizing one or another, or even different combinations, of these four basic themes. Nonetheless, all of the essays in this book have one basic concern in common: the

---

[1] I am using the expression "male love" here as a shorthand for "male-male love," that is, for the love between men.

role religion and ethics play in the literary depiction and understanding of male love. In some cases we shall see that male love is straightforwardly and positively depicted in religious literature; in other cases it is portrayed only metaphorically, or through the use of other rhetorical devices. In other cases still, religion is used as an interpretive device: at times it is used in this way by the author of a secular literary work—religion itself then becomes the rhetorical strategy used to understand male love; in other instances religion, or one aspect of it (ethics or mysticism, for example), becomes the interpretive strategy for the critic or scholar who seeks to understand the depiction of male love in a religious or secular work. But regardless of the variety of the permutations and the complexity of the problems, the essays that follow have a basic threefold focus—religion, homosexuality and literature.

Comstock, for example, suggests in "Love Power and Competition Among Men in 1 and 2 Samuel: Jonathan as Unconventional Nurturer," that the author of the biblical material he is dealing with, might have used a relatively neutral rhetoric of covenant, friendship, elegy and so forth to encode for his audience a message whose literal exposition—the mutual love of Jonathan and David—would have been unacceptable. At the same time he suggests that the code itself may have been one that was understood "by gay men with a recognizing ear." If Comstock is right, this indicates that the author of these biblical passages found literary ways—codes—to escape the restrictions imposed on him by a society that was intolerant of the type of love he was attempting to portray. He found a way to sympathetically depict the fact and character of male love, as well as Jonathan's possession of what was not a stereotypical male quality, that of being a nurturer, through ingenious and recognizable literary devices that were understood only by those for whom it was intended.

Interestingly, we find a similar scenario suggested by the second essay, Kripal's "Ramakrishna's Foot: Mystical Homoeroticism in the *Kathāmṛta*." Ramakrishna, a nineteenth century Bengali Hindu saint and mystic, is a far cry from the Jonathan of the Hebrew Bible; and there are few points in common between the author of 1 and 2 Samuel and Gupta, the author of the *Kathāmṛta*, a five volume compilation on the life and teachings of Ramakrishna during the last five years of his life. But Kripal shows that the *Kathāmṛta* is structured so as to conceal Ramakrishna's secret, the passion he has for his boy disciples, and that in the *Kathāmṛta*

Gupta, the author, uses a variety of rhetorical strategies to gloss over Ramakrishna's otherwise overtly homoerotic visions and pronouncements. Kripal's main point, however, has to do neither with the author of the *Kathāmṛta* nor with its English translator, who, incidentally, simply left the "offending" passages of the text untranslated. Instead it has to do with Ramakrishna himself, and with his own self-perception. Kripal suggests that religion—specifically a combination of the erotic imagery to be found in the *bhakti* (devotional) and tantric traditions—gave Ramakrishna a hermeneutic, albeit unacknowledged, for accepting and legitimizing the love he felt for boys. Hence, his love for Purna becomes conflated with the "anxious longing" for God, his taking on the role of Kṛṣṇa's consort, Radha, allows him to engage with men as if he were a women, and the spontaneity of mystical fervor allows him and his disciples to shed their garments and dance. In this sense perhaps Gupta's "spiritualizing" rhetoric that reads religious meaning into Ramakrishna's homoeroticism is nothing more than the literary counterpart of Ramakrishna's own internal rhetoric, one that allowed him to express the love he had for his disciples while concealing his secret "even from himself."

Kripal's *Kathāmṛta* provides us, then, with a religious reading of homoeroticism in what is essentially a biographical and historical work. The biblical texts that are the principal sources of Comstock's work provide us with what might be termed a military and political reading of homosexual love in a religious text. Now the Japanese *kana zoshi* literature extols explicitly sexual love between men as a means to ethical development.

Finally, Vitiello's "Taoist Themes in Chinese Homoerotic Tales" is an analysis of a variety of Chinese literary texts, including the famous *Cut Sleeve*. There we will find an intermediary position between the rhetoric of concealment found in the Hebrew Bible and the encomium of the *kana zoshi*. Vitiello's point, it seems to me, is that, except for certain physiological considerations involving the transfer of semen (the essential and vital force whose presence is required for health and even immortality according to Taoist metaphysics), male homosexual love is essentially neutral to the task of religious cultivation. Only when it involves excess that leads to a breakdown in propriety or, more importantly, to the loss of the adept's semen, is male love brought into question. It is not, however, the homosexual nature of the liaison itself that is condemned, for a similar critique is made of heterosexual relations that involve such excess. Hence, at the very least, the Taoist attitude toward male love, as reflected in these tales, is one of neutrality.

Taken as a whole, the papers raise a number of interesting questions. We shall witness in the essays that follow at least two forms of what might be termed a "rhetoric of concealment." One involves a military and political reading of this male love, another a religious reading of it. What other interpretive strategies have been utilized to conceal the fact and character of the love between men? Also, in what sense do these rhetorical devices actually conceal? Surely they do no conceal to the point of making the secret of male love totally unavailable to their audiences (both Comstock and Kripal agree on this). Might it then be the case that such rhetorical strategies are simply the motions that texts must go through to make acceptable the unacceptable?

To proceed farther east: is there even in East Asia a masking of male love in military, political or religious terms? Although Schalow's *kana zoshi* literature does utilize Buddhist doctrinal principles to eulogize homosexual love, it is hardly a masking. Clearly, a rhetoric of masking or concealment is necessary only in situations where male love is considered socially unacceptable, which is neither the case in medieval Japan nor in Classical China.

Turning the tables, is religion ever used as a force legitimizing homosexual love in Western literature, religious or secular? Are there any cases where the same-sex nature of the love is considered neutral in regard to the question of religious and ethical cultivation; or if it *is* subversive of the religious norm, only as subversive as heterosexual love?

These, it seems to me, are questions that these essays ask of each other, but what do they ask and say to us? First and foremost they speak to us of the multivocality of the gay experience. They tell us that there have been other times and places when gay men (and women) felt they had to hide the expression of their love for one another. And yet, there have been other times and places where moral and religious ideals and same sex love have either been neutral to each other, or have actually been used to mutually legitimize and bolster the other. Just as there have been other times and places where the religious life has not been antithetical to being gay, so might we hope that there will once again exist such times in our own culture. This is the gift of the historical and cross-cultural study of gay experience: it is a gift of hope in the face of oppression.

I would like to conclude by offering some general remarks on the study of gay cultures within the religious studies academy. There appears to me to exist a dangerous polarization in the treatment of religion and homosexuality, a polarization that is leading to the devaluation of rigorous academic and scholarly study in favor of more popular politically advocative work. I reject this dichotomy because I believe that work that lacks scholarly rigor is ultimately ineffective politically, and that truly scholarly work is creative in such a way that it must of necessity have implications in a political sphere.

There must be room, not only for many approaches, but for many different voices—including voices from different places and times. The academic study of religion and homosexuality must continue to reflect the diversity of the gay experience itself. It must be methodologically diverse and cross-cultural in nature. To the extent that the field has headed in that direction it should be encouraged. When it becomes methodologically, culturally or racially parochial it must be corrected. Gay studies, especially in the religious studies academy, is in its infancy. How sad it would be if diversity were not nurtured within it while the opportunity exists.

Inclusivity must be the rule, but this need not be achieved at the price of scholarly rigor. If there is one thing that will insure the long-term political effectiveness of our scholarship, it is excellence. This is something that has never been lacking in the gay community, scholarly or otherwise, and it is something certainly not lacking in the four outstanding essays that make up this book.

III. Gary David Comstock

Love, Power and Competition Among Men in Hebrew Scripture: Jonathan as Unconventional Nurturer

Introduction

Within 1 Samuel, Jonathan makes six appearances: in chapter 13 he strikes down the pillar of the Philistines at Geba; in chapter 14 he is a heroic warrior at Michmash; in chapter 18 he makes a covenant with David; in chapter 19 he warns David of Saul's anger; in chapter 20 he advises David to flee from Saul; and in chapter 23 he goes to and comforts David in the wilderness. In addition, in chapter 22 Saul refers to "my son" as making "a league with the son of Jesse ... against me;" and in chapter 31 Jonathan is mentioned as dying alongside Saul and his two other sons in battle. Within 2 Samuel, a messenger announces and David laments Jonathan's death in chapter 1; Jonathan's son, Meribbaal, is introduced in chapter 4 as having fled and become crippled after the defeat of Saul; David welcomes Meribbaal into his house in chapter 9; the servant of Meribbaal betrays his loyalty to David in chapter 16; Meribbaal demonstrates his loyalty to David in chapter 19; and David spares the life of Meribbaal and recovers and buries the bones of Saul and Jonathan in chapter 21.

Jonathan is an unusual character; and commentators have had difficulty accepting him. They have assigned labels and characteristics to him that he does not warrant, and they have overlooked those qualities which make him unique. Scholars for the most part have been uncomfortable with Jonathan. Perhaps Jobling is most honest when he finds Jonathan's "attitudes and actions lacking any normal motivation."[1]

Jonathan is usually viewed as King Saul's son and "rightful successor" who "voluntarily waive[s] his right to the throne in favor of David."[2] The story of David and Jonathan is usually understood as Jonathan's acquiescence to David's kingship.[3] This understanding is predicated on Jonathan's being at the height of his career as a military leader[4] and on his being the heir apparent to Saul's throne. The text, however, supports neither reading.

Rebel Warrior

The image of Jonathan in 1 Samuel 13 and 14 is less that of the heroic military leader and more that of the rebel or unconventional warrior and son. Jonathan's action in 1 Samuel 13:3 is usually translated as having "defeated the garrison of the Philistines at Geba" (RSV), but following the meaning of **neṣîb** from 1 Samuel 10:5, Jonathan's action in chapter 13 should be understood as against a "pillar," perhaps a "prefect," but not a "garrison," for which **maṣṣāb** is more common (1 Samuel 13:23; 14:1, 4, 6, 11, 12, 15.). The reason for reading "pillar" also rests on the consequence of the action. A great military victory is not noted, nor is concrete damage done; but the Philistines are effectively annoyed. His striking down the pillar at Geba does not give Israel a military advantage, but creates literally "a bad odor" (1 Samuel 13:4, **bā'as**) in the noses of the Philistines and provokes retaliation for which Israel is not prepared. Pedersen notes that knocking over such a pillar would have been more than sufficient to inaugurate a retaliatory war, which is what happens in chapter 14.[5]

His subsequent exploit at Michmash (1 Samuel 14) is not much greater. Jonathan attacks a weakened post; his plan is sudden and not well-considered; his success depends to a large extent on his armor-bearer; together they kill only twenty. The ensuing battle in which the men of Israel join is neither great nor conclusive. Jonathan as a warrior is impulsive, risky, individualistic, inspirational. While popular, he is not a leader, but rather one who is respected for his bravery and unconventionality.[6]

Kirkpatrick writes: "When I Samuel opens at the end of the period of the judges, Israel appears as a loose congeries of tribes, united by their common allegiance to Yahweh, and capable from time to time under temporary leaders of common action, but powerless to resist the dominant power in Palestine. When II Samuel closes, the tribes have been welded into a powerful nation."[7] Jonathan is such a temporary military leader who abdicates such an ineffective kind of leadership to one who would lead differently and more effectively. Jonathan is a warrior who faces an ominous military obstacle against which he lacks the preparation and capability to fight, and who consequently recognizes David's qualifications to lead. That he has the good sense to give up military leadership seems to be to his credit. Saul, on the other hand, does not change with the times.

Person of Yahweh

While Jonathan's military performance in 1 Samuel 14 is not notable for leadership, body count, or strategic outcome, the directness of his relationship with Yahweh does stand out. The thoroughness with which Saul performs cultic activities and consults priests is in sharp contrast with Jonathan's disobeying his father and approaching Yahweh directly without consulting the priests.[8] Jonathan breaks fast, ritual, and rule without fear of consequences (1 Samuel 14:28-35). Not only is he not harmed when he violates rules, he seems to be rewarded—e.g., he is rescued by the people in 1 Samuel 14:45 and his "eyes are brightened" by breaking the fast in 1 Samuel 14:27.[9] Jonathan (his name meaning "Yahweh has given")[10] is victorious, not because he has won a battle or led Israel, but "because he has been at work with God today" (1 Sam 14:45). He even speaks for Yahweh: "For Yahweh has given them into the hand of Israel" (1 Sam 14:12). Whereas one expects here, following from v.10, to read "into our hand," the narrative seems to present with intentional juxtaposition "into the hand of Israel," as Yahweh would speak but on the lips of Jonathan.[11] Jonathan's battle is identical with Yahweh's battle and is in Yahweh's complete control. In 1 Sam 14:15 the initial "panic in the camp" soon becomes "divine panic," **tehî leḥerddat 'elohîm**. The victory is Yahweh's performance, neither Israel's nor Jonathan's (1 Sam 14:23.).[12] Hertzberg recognizes as central to the story not outcomes but the overriding influence of Yahweh as preserved from the old material by the hand of the Deuteronomistic compiler.[13]

Jobling suggests that there are in 1 Samuel 14 three basic traditions that originally had no connection to each other, and, though not negative toward Saul by themselves, in their placement with each other and through the structuring of 1 Samuel 13 through 15, they are. The redaction of 1 Sam 14:1-46 tends to diminish Saul and exalt Jonathan.[14] I would point out that it does more than develop their individual characters; 1 Samuel 14 establishes, also, the pattern of Saul's relationship with Jonathan which is repeated in three of the other Jonathan chapters, 1 Samuel 18, 19, and 20. In all four, subsequent to an activity of Jonathan, which is noticeable for its unconventionality, is Saul's disapproval, which is noticeable for its anger, ignorance or narrow-mindedness. While it is argued by most commentators that Saul's displeasure with Jonathan in 1 Samuel 18 and subsequently is caused or provoked by Jonathan's supposed acquiescence to David's kingship, the pattern of Saul's displeasure with Jonathan is established well before that issue surfaces in the narrative. This pattern for Jonathan and Saul's relationships as well as Jonathan's prominent and distinguishing characteristic as a person of Yahweh are firmly in place as Jonathan makes his third appearance in 1 Samuel 18.

COVENANT MAKER

Jonathan, the one who had acted with Yahweh in battle in 1 Samuel 14 becomes the maker of a covenant with David in 1 Samuel 18. Thompson, in attempt to undermine the centrality and primacy of the covenant, says that it "was only one of many covenants of one kind or another which were made over the years until David was finally securely established to the throne."[15] But of the eleven times in which some form of or reference to covenant-making occurs in 1 and 2 Samuel, eight have to do with the David-Jonathan covenant.[16]

And while Jobling and Kirkpatrick insist that the **berît 'ôlām,** "eternal covenant," of "the last words of David," in 2 Sam 23:5 refers to "the everlasting dynasty" which Yahweh wills David to build in 2 Sam 7:12-16,[17] the terms customarily used to name such an agreement and promise, **kārat** and **berît,** are not present in this latter passage. They are, however, used repeatedly in the David-Jonathan covenant passages, and the term **'ôlām**, "eternal," modifies them (1 Sam 20:8, 15, 23).

HEIR APPARENT?

Efforts to minimize the David-Jonathan covenant and regard it simply as an aid to David in his pursuit of the kingship rely on the assumption that Jonathan is the heir apparent to Saul's kingship and gives up his position to David.[18] And yet, for the following reasons, I find that the narrative assumes neither male lineage nor dynastic succession.

[1] Prior to David's appearance in the narrative and prior to the forming of David and Jonathan's relationship, Samuel tells Saul twice that his kingship has already ended (1 Sam 13:13-14; 15:11-35).

[2] Nowhere in the narrative is there any indication from Jonathan of his expectations to be king.[19]

[3] Saul's vow to let Jonathan's life be taken in 1 Sam 14:42 and his "casting his spear to smite him" in 1 Sam 20:33 would suggest that Saul neither expected or seriously wanted Jonathan to succeed him.

[4] There is only one instance in the narrative (1 Sam 20:33-31) where Saul speaks to Jonathan about succeeding him and it is a passing reference made in the midst of insults and an emotional outburst. Furthermore, the term used here, **malkût**, can mean "royal power" or "royal dignity," as well as "kingship." It does not have the more precise and singular meaning of **melûkā**, used by Samuel in 1 Sam 10:25 to designate Saul's position and rank as Israel's first king.[20]

[5] If Jonathan is the heir apparent, why cannot a brother take his place when he defaults? Patrilineal kingship is not typically restricted to the oldest son. Saul has other sons who could have succeeded him.[21]

[6] The transferring of clothes from Jonathan to David in 1 Sam 18:4 is read by some commentators as symbolizing the transfer of kingship.[22] Goldman's comment, however, that Jonathan's **me'îl**, "robe," indicates "high rank"[23] would suggest that it is not first and foremost a kingly or even royal robe.[24] The robe's being given with Jonathan's armor, sword, bow and belt, would suggest that if any office or rank is being transferred, it is military, not royal, and this would be supported both by the development of Jonathan's character in 1 Samuel 13 and 14 and by David's success in leading soldiers immediately following in vs. 5, 6-7, 13-16. Because commentators focus, for the most part, so singularly on succession and kingship in 1 and 2 Samuel, they view the transfer or abdication in 1 Sam 18:1-5 as Royal rather than as military, in spite of the passage's emphasis on the weapons.

[7] Jobling makes a case for Jonathan's being "presented unmistakable as king [in 1 Samuel 20] ... during Saul's temporary indisposition [at Ramah]" by pointing out: (a) that Jonathan

speaks as a king, **ḥolîlâ lo' tāmôt**, "far from it!," in 1 Sam 20:2, as Saul did in 1 Sam 19:6; (b) that in 1 Sam 20:41 David treats Jonathan as a king by doing obeisance; and (c) that David enters "the presence," **pānîm**, of Jonathan in 1 Sam 16:21,22; 17:57; and 19:7.[25] However, the term **ḥolîlâ** does not indicate precisely kingly authority as much as authority characterized by certainty; e.g., in 1 Sam 14:45 "the people" use the term to inform Saul that Jonathan is not to die.[26] Furthermore, doing obeisance was the custom of an oriental when he met a superior (e.g., Gen 33:3), and the superior did not have to be the highest official (e.g., in Gen 42:6 Joseph is governor, not Pharaoh).[27] And finally, Jonathan would not have to be king to have someone come "before" him. He could simply be a person of high rank, the king's son.[28] But Jobling's observation here of the association with Jonathan of a term which has been associated with Saul previously in the narrative is convincing. However, the term may be used less to signal a shift of kingly status from Saul to Jonathan and more a shift in Jonathan and David's relationship. David for the first time comes to and needs Jonathan. Later, when Jonathan goes to David in the wilderness (1 Sam 23:15-18), it is neither as future king nor subject. Even though Jonathan tells David that David will be king, Jonathan also says "I shall be next to you" (RSV).[29] The inequality within their relationship is underscored when the **pānîm** term is used in v. 18, but for "the two of them," **senehem**, to make a covenant "before" Yahweh.

[8] We need, also, to ask if anything in 2 Samuel requires to establishes Jonathan as the heir apparent or kingship as patrilineal; and the following suggest not:

[a] David grieves Saul's and Jonathan's deaths and avenges the assassination of Saul's son Ishbaal (2 Sam 1:15ff.; 4:9-12; 21:11-14). He does not play a part in having them killed. However, when David is directly involved in wiping out the house of Saul, i.e., when he knows that Saul's offspring are being killed and has a hand in it (2 Sam 21:7-9), those who are killed are the sons of Saul's daughter, or, stated another way, the sons of Saul's wife's daughter.

[b] David's other direct action that could be interpreted as cutting off a ruling line—and this would also be matrilineal—may be his refusal to have children with Saul's daughter, Michal (2 Sam 6:23), and his preventing her from having children with her husband (2 Sam 3:12-16).

[c] If by patrilineal descent, Saul's house were to rule, David would not have spared Meribbaal, the son of Jonathan, the supposed former heir apparent (2 Samuel 9).

[d] There is no mention in 2 Samuel by any of Saul's descendants that they aspired to rule. Ishbaal, Saul's other son, is not an active participant in the war against David, but one who obeys David (2 Sam 3:14-15).[30]

[e] One may reasonably ask why, if male lineage was not assumed, 2 Samuel spends time describing the ending of Saul's house. If we look at the ending of Saul's house through the killing of his concubine's sons and his daughter's sons, the account is actually very brief, functioning more as an appendix than as an integrated part of the story. And Ishbaal's story occupies noticeably space more as Abner's story than as his own. Ishbaal is buried in Abner's tomb and never re-located to rest with Saul and his other sons (2 Sam 21:14). Also, Ishbaal's assassins state as their motif not the ending of assumed threats to David's rule or claim to the throne, but the avenging of Saul's attempt on David's life (2 Sam 4:8).[31]

[g] The only explicit suggestion about restoring Saul's kingdom patrilineally is spoken not by a son but by a servant of Saul (2 Sam 16:3). The term for "kingdom" here, **malkût**, is the same used in 1 Sam 20:30, which, as discussed previously, does not have the specific meaning of "kingship" as does **melûkā**.

[h] In 2 Sam 19:28 Meribbaal recognizes and states that he has no right to the throne. Patrilineal access is not even entertained as a possibility.[32] Meribbaal's life is preserved by David because of **ḥesed** for Jonathan (note the repetition of the term in the short 2 Sam 9:1-7 passage), not because of any claim to the throne. Since 2 Sam 9:1-7 is generally considered part of the "Early source" material, noted for its "sober objectivity" by a writer who "was obviously dealing with events of which he had personal knowledge and in which he may have participated,"[33] we may assume that Meribbaal's indifference to seeking the throne as depicted here reflects the conventions of lineage-rule, i.e., not patrilineal, during his time in history.[34]

PERSONAL FRIEND AND LOVER

Efforts are also made by commentators to undermine the *personal* aspect of the David-Jonathan covenant. Thompson, for example, says that in 1 Sam 18:1-5:

> The narrator uses the ambiguous word *love* (**'aheb**) because it denoted more than natural affection however deep and genuine this may have been. ... In this context, ... it denotes rather the kind of attachment people had to a king who could fight their battles for them.[35]

But in his attempt to view the David-Jonathan relationship politically he does not mention other references to their relationship which use terms of attraction of a non-political nature, e.g., **ḥofeṣ**, "delighted much in" (1 Sam 19:1); **māṣā'tîḥen**, "have found favor in your eyes" (1 Sam 20:3); **hanne'îmim**, "lovely" (2 Sam 1 :23); and **nā'amttālî me'od**, "very dear to me" (2 Sam 1:26). Also, while he argues that a verb customarily used to express personal love, set in a covenant-making and/or political context, becomes political, he does not allow for the reverse, a conventional political context, like covenant-making, being used to express, perhaps covertly, a deep and possibly prohibited or unconventional interpersonal love.

Three aspects of the 1 Sam 18:1-5 covenant make it special, unique, and noteworthy. First, the term **kenaffeso**, "as his own self," in vs. 1 and 3 ("Jonathan loved David as his own self") is used elsewhere in making vassal-lord agreements, but it is found also in Deut 13:6 (MT 7) to qualify the word for **re'a**, "friend" ("Your friend who is as your own self").[36] Missing from the Deuteronomy phrasing in Samuel 18 is **re'a**, replaced, however, by the verb to love, **'āhab**. Not only is the term **kenaffeso** with **'āhab** repeated in b. 3, it is given as the only reason for the making of the covenant. It perhaps alters what may have been a more formulaic or conventional expression for friend.

Secondly, the word **qāsar**, "to knit," in v. 1 ("the whole self of Jonathan was to knit to the whole self of David") is used elsewhere in Hebrew scripture, but infrequently, to express profound intimacy or closeness (e.g., Gen 44:30; Isa 49:18). If the Deut 13:6 (MT 7) passage reflects or suggests a basis for the language in 1 Sam 18:1-5, it should also be noted that it uses term for "clinging to," **dābaq**, and its object is Yahweh. The term **qāsar** in 1 Sam 18:1-5, however, has the more participatory, interacting, sharing, and conspiring sense of bonding,[37] as might be required by covenant-making between equals.

Thirdly, as Driber notes, conventional covenant-making formula and terminology are altered in 1 Sam 18:1-5. Because Jonathan is the subject to the end of v. 3, the **waw** with David is read by some commentators as **lamed**. But **lamed** is only in rare exceptions used and only of a superior (e.g., Ezra 10:3 and 2 Chr 29:10), usually a conqueror prescribing terms for an inferior (e.g., 1 Sam 11:1; Judg 2:2; and Isa 55:32), which is unsuitable here. The difficulty in reading the text as it appears may suggest that the conventional form of covenant-making was not suitable for the needs and purposes of the Jonathan-David relationship, and had to be modified. Harrelson notes that "friendship, of this sort was a rare thing between equals of different family backgrounds." Driver's observations that the **ye'ehābeô** in 1 Sam 18:1 is a rare form of **'āhab** and that the repeated **'ad**, "and even" of 1 Sam 18:14 b, is emphatic would seem to recognize also the unusualness, both in terms of grammar and content, of the passage. The term **pāsat**, "to strip," of 1 Sam 18:4a, suggests a maximum or extreme de-clothing, and establishes further the passage's quality of going-beyond-the-usual.[38] The unconventional warrior and rebellious son of 1 Samuel 13 and 14 continues to be unconventional in friendship and love. And while Saul may initially approve of the object of Jonathan's affection (1 Sam 18:2), as he did of Jonathan's initial military exploits (1 Sam 13:3), he soon disapproves and is frustrated (1 Sam 18:8), as he was subsequent to the battle at Michmash Pass (1 Sam 14:29, 44).

JONATHAN'S LOVE, YAHWEH'S ACTION

While similarities to the terms in Deuteronomy 13 have been noted, more needs to be said of that passage's content. Its warnings against idolatry, against rebellion against Yahweh, may have their counterpart in 1 Sam 18:1-5. Noticeably, Yahweh's name is absent in 1 Samuel 18, but the terms for "love" and "knit" are conspicuous. After 1 Samuel 18, the covenant with Jonathan is referred to as "of" or "before Yahweh" (1 Sam 20:8, 23; 23:18; 2

Sam 21:7). Jonathan speaks to David with Yahweh's authority in 1 Sam 20:13, and in 1 Sam 23:15-18 is the first one to tell David that he will be king. In the later passage, Jonathan goes to David in the wilderness to "strengthen his [David's] hand in God," and the two of them make "a covenant before Yahweh." Furthermore, if David is consistently faithful to anything throughout 1 and 2 Samuel, it is to his love for Jonathan. In 2 Sam 9:1 the "kindness for Jonathan's sake" that David wishes to show to "any one of the house of Saul," is expressed soon after as "the kindness of God," v. 3.

Yahweh is basic to this covenant. To Saul, pious and concerned for his position as king, it makes no sense. He interprets it in 1 Sam 20:30 as perversity, rebellion, preference for companionship that is anti-familial. Saul sees David and Jonathan's relationship as "a league" against him (1 Sam 22:8), and misses again, as he did as the pious observer of priestly ritual in 1 Samuel 13 and 14 Jonathan's activities seem to fly in the face of priestliness, in 1 Sam 22:6-8 his relationship with David flies in the face of principalities, territorial aggrandizement, and tribal rivalries that threaten Israel's unity. Jonathan here stands outside of Saul's court as he did outside of the altars, rules, and ritual sacrifices in 1 Samuel 14. Sitting "under the tamarisk tree on the height, with his spear in his hand" as a judge, Saul maintains an outdated method of leadership and continues to stir up tribal rivalries.[39]

Some commentators have interpreted their covenant either as (1) the beginning of the divine promise of kingship which replace the inadequate former priesthood and military leadership[40] or as (2) representing the Deuteronomistic concept of deliverance which depends on fidelity to Yahweh.[41] But, that which is explicit in the text and basic to their covenant is the love between two people outside of family, tribe and convention.

While Gunn maintains that "theologically speaking it is Jonathan who justifies Yaweh's action,"[42] we need to be clear what is meant by Yahweh's action. Gunn sees it as establishing the kingship. I see it as establishing love between people. Perhaps it is both. But more to the point is that Yahweh's action is Jonathan's love and commitment to David, which is not the same as seeing Yahweh's promise as that of a Davidic kingship. The narrative in no way leads us to read that Jonathan tries to make David king or that he loves David because David will or should be king. Jonathan even loves David before he kills his ten-thousands. Jonathan loves the person David. Kennedy notes the "humanness and secularity" of David's lament for Jonathan (2 Sam 1:19-27);[43] and Driver comments that "it is remarkable that no religious thought of any kind appears in the poem: the feeling expressed by it is purely human."[44] I would place the meaning of the Jonathan-David covenant in human love, as does Moran who writes: "The conception of profane love is analogous to the love of God in Deuteronomy, [a love] that can [also] be commanded, ... a covenantal love."[45]

In the context of vying for territory and control, Jonathan and David's covenant, based on **'āhab**, makes no sense politically. Neither one has much to give the other in the material sense. They do not fight each other's military battles; Jonathan actually stays with and fights alongside of Saul (1 Sam 20:42; 23:18; 31:2, 6), and David deliberately avoids and does not attack Saul (1 Samuel 24 and 26). They conspire to love each other and keep each other safe; they do not conspire to gain power or to overthrow Saul. They aid each other less in terms of providing material support and more in terms of nurture. They are there for each other at the most difficult times—Jonathan for David when his safety is most threatened by Saul; and for each other when they are forced to separate (1 Sam 19:1-7; 20:1ff.; 23:15-18).

THE CHARACTER OF JONATHAN

Jonathan's significance for us lies precisely in the way that commentators dismiss him in terms of his "naivete and simplistic view of good and evil" as does Gunn,[46] or as "not normal, flat, static, certainly opaque" as does Jobling,[47] while refusing to recognize him as the interesting and complex character he is, one who is unconventional pushy, and aggressive as well as gentle, calm and nurturing. It is this later image of Jonathan as lover or nurturer which nudges readers to accept uncomfortably a man with motives other than material and political success, a man who stands by his man for love not gain.

Although Jonathan is unconventional, it is his constancy—both in his love for David and in his loyalty to Saul—that gives his character depth. Jonathan affects David and Saul, but he is never the force which gives either the edge or advantage over the other. Within the highly competitive and conflictual relationships within 1 and 2 Samuel, Jonathan's love for and relationship with David is present and insists, but is not casual. Jonathan is a nurturer, not a "main player." Against the scheming, deception, and contest, Jonathan establishes an intimate, nurturing, vulnerable relationship which promises no political gain. The body of scholarship which reads into the story Jonathan's acquiescence to David's kingship may be an attempt to rationalize the disbelief and annoyance that straight men feel, but cannot reasonably explain, when confronted by non-threatening, intimate, loving relationships between men. The traditional interpretation of Jonathan as one who has the power to yield the throne, and the accompanying evaluation of his character as flat, weak and unrealistic because he gives up such power, is the product, I think, of a dominant heterosexual male hermeneutic. Gay men, especially those who have risked coming out in some or all aspects of their lives, more readily recognize and credit human love and not politics as the arena of David and Jonathan's relationship; and we do not flinch when Jonathan risks social security for personal affection.

Commentators tend to react to Meribbaal as they do to Jonathan. Meribbaal's response to David in 2 Sam 9:8 is often seen as exaggerated, even in terms of Eastern manners.[48] His seemingly exaggerated politeness and devotion, however, mirror or complement Jonathan's friendship, unselfishness and dedication. The narrative does not present these characters unconsciously. They are presented in such a way as to require a response—to make us want to dismiss or not to take seriously their straightforward, non-manipulative relationships with David. The narrative itself contains incidents of irritation with these unmanly men; not only Saul in 1 Sam 20:30 with Jonathan, but David himself in 2 Sam 16:4 has to decide whether or not Meribbaal is sincere. And he does not do well. Goldman suggests that the narrator, by emphasizing David's response in 2 Samuel 16:4, "thine is all," draws our attention to David's becoming accustomed to the enormous ingratitude surrounding him at the time, which Meribbaal will puncture dramatically with its opposite in Sam 19:24-30.[49] Commentators split on whether or not Meribbaal's mourning is genuine.[50] The narrative has this built-in device which tests the reader's willingness or ability to accept or believe in this covenant of Yahweh.

The anomaly of 1 Samuel is Jonathan's leaning to David. The anomaly of 2 Samuel is David's leaning to Meribbaal. That David befriends Meribbaal makes little sense, of course. The political advantage is minimal. Meribbaal is neither in a position to advance nor challenge David. Whereas 1 Sam 18:1-5 hinges on **'āhab**, 2 Sam 9:1-7 hinges on **ḥesed**. It is not kindness which is material payment. Like **'āhab** in Sam 18:1-5, **ḥesed** in 2 Sam 9:1-7 is repeated for emphasis. While 1 Sam 18:1-5 features the gift-giving aspect of covenant-making, 2 Sam 9:1-7 features the covenantal meal. In 1 Sam 18:1-5 the repeated **'ad**, "and even," emphasizes the gift-giving, while 2 Sam 9:1-7 **tāmîd**, "always," emphasizes the meal and reflects the **'ôlām** of the "eternal covenant" of 2 Sam 23:5 and 1 Sam 20:23, 42. Together 1 Sam 18:1-5 and Sam 9:1-7 include a complementary range of covenant-making elements. The covenant, as initiated by Jonathan and extended by David to Meribbaal, is a complete, cohesive unit, while at the same time, as discussed above, it has features which are unique.

CAMOUFLAGED LOVER?

But why must the Jonathan-David relationship be set in the context of a covenant? If they were not political rivals in need of resolving problems, why the covenant form? Why not simply speak of their love as Michal's love is spoken of in 1 Sam 18:20? It may hold up theological values about love and friendship. The covenant may have been used to give the relationship importance and notice. Since their relationship was not a treaty, an oath, or a league, its special meaning may have found an appropriate mode of expression in the recognized sacredness of the covenant before Yahweh. Or, the covenant may have been a convenient form for saying something that could not be said another way. Some observations about genre and motif may help further our understanding of the use of covenant here.

Joseph Cady in his work on Walt Whitman states that gay writers writing in a time that is hostile to gay people had to invent protective strategies that would allow them to express themselves while sufficiently guarding themselves against social exposure and punishment.[51]

Cady goes on to say that gay writers in nineteenth-century American and Great Britain made imaginative expropriations from existing popular frameworks, adapting terms which they felt were also applicable to or potentially true about the homosexual bond. Such a term for Whitman was "adhesion," which he borrowed from a popular movement during his time known as phrenology. Other terms involved the language of "friendship" and comradeship."[52] If the situation for gay writers at the time of the Deuteronomist was similar, such appropriate terms might have been **kenaffeso** or **qāsar**, typical covenant terms, words like **'āhab** from politics, or a slight altering of such terms, as noted in Driver's discussion of the **lamed** with David's name in 1 Sam 18:3. Such coding and camouflaging of terms would have been heard by other gay men with a recognizing ear.[53]

Cady states further that a common convention in nineteenth century male homosexual literature was the elegy, which was an effective cover permitting intense and open expression of love because the praised one was, after all, dead. Another convention was "soldier-comradeship," even less discernible than ordinary "comradeship" since men were together not by preference and the absence of women required their tending to one another.[54]

Such invention could have occurred in the 1 and 2 Samuel narrative. I am not saying that the particular inventions of nineteenth-century American gay writers would have been the same as those of the writers in biblical times. In each period, gay writers would make use of what was available and extend it accordingly. I would add, however, although I have not referred to it yet, that David's lament for Jonathan in 2 Samuel 1 fits the "elegy" and "soldier-comrade" vehicles too perfectly not at least to mention. As an accepted literary convention the lament or elegy would not have aroused suspicion. The sharing of attention between Saul and Jonathan provides a good cover (how many have pointed out that David owed none of those comments to Saul?), and terms like **nā'îm**, "pleasant," in 2 Sam 1:23, 26 have erotic associations (cf., Cant 1:16), as well as the safety of fraternal association (cf., Ps 133:1).[55] Problems that have occurred traditionally in translating certain words, such as **qāset**, "bow," in 2 Sam 1:18 and **ṣebî**, "glory" or "gazelle" in 2 Sam 1:19, may for a gay man present clear signals and less of an obstacle. The "bow" could refer quite easily to Jonathan, since the bow was a gift of their covenant (1 Sam 20:35-42). The possible double meaning of **ṣebî** lest a gay man favor "gazelle" to refer to and remember the Jonathan who swiftly crossed mountain ranges to visit David in his time of need (1 Sam 23:15-18). Such a coded introductory reference—along with the concluding reference to David's love for Jonathan (2 Sam 1:26)—allows for a camouflaged framing of the entire lament in favor of Jonathan, while preserving the explicitly balanced homage to Saul and Jonathan's son later in the narrative would provide the ultimate cover.

CONCLUSION

The conventional and socially acceptable language and form of covenant, friendship, politics, elegy, and soldiering may have been used to tell a love story which needed both to remain within what was socially acceptable as well as to break with convention, that is, to tell a story that would appeal to and be heard differently by two different audiences.

I have read the arguments for whether or not homosexuality was practiced at the time and in the place of Jonathan and David and specifically by them. The argument that most cultures in the ancient Near East allowed homosexual practices is not convincing to me because the counter-argument can always be made that basic to Israel was Yahweh's admonition and its endeavor to be unlike its neighbors. At any rate, I doubt that homosexuality was socially accepted during most of biblical times. But I assume that gay or homosexually-orientated people did exist and I am interested in their efforts to express themselves. It is less important to me that David and Jonathan, the historical figures themselves, might have had a homosexual relationship than that a gay writer or writers may have used an available framework that would be read by other gay men as a gay story, but not as such by non-gay people.[56]

For gay men today, then, Jonathan may be embraced as a fellow lover. We identify with Jonathan and the writers of his story. We find strength for ourselves not because the story tells us how to live, but because the story shows that others lived through similar problems and struggled to assert themselves as we have done. We grasp from the very existence of Jonathan's story and how it came to be told support for our won struggle. Against the objections of his father, but with the blessing of his god and his feelings of affection, Jonathan builds and sustains a loving relationship with David. Within 1 and 2 Samuel the Jonathan story engages the larger narrative to point to needed social changes in military, political, and religious organization. The Jonathan who emerges in this story and in the larger narrative is unconventional in love, in war, as a son, as a man. Within the social context within which Jonathan's story was compiled and written, I would suggest that gay writers were able to include his story as a message and signal to other gay men who seek an alternative to business as usual.

---

[1] David Jobling, *The Sense of Biblical Narrative: Three Structural Analyses in the Old Testament (1 Samuel 13-31, Numbers 11-12, 1 Kings 17-18)* (Sheffield: JSOT, 1978), p. 20.

[2] Norman K. Gottwald, *The Hebrew Bible—A Socio-Literary Introduction* (Philadelphia: Fortress, 1985), p. 315.

[3] See David M. Gunn, *The Fate of King Saul: An Interpretation of a Biblical Story* (Sheffield: JSOT, 1980), pp. 14, 80, 81, 84, 93, 120; Peter R. Ackroyd, *The First Book of Samuel* (London: Cambridge University Press, 1971), pp. 147, 167; and Jobling (1978), pp. 13-14.

[4] See, for example, Hans Wilhelm Hertzberg, *I and II Samuel: A Commentary*, trans. J.S. Bowden (Philadelphia: Westminster Press, 1964), p. 132; and Jobling (1978), p. 12.

[5] Johannes Pedersen, *Israel: Its Life and Culture* (London: Oxford University Press, 1926; reprinted, 1954) I-II, p. 25. See, also: A.F. Kirkpatrick, *The First and Second Books of Samuel* (London: Cambridge University Press, 1889; revised 1930), p. 436; and W.O. E. Oesterley, *The First Book of Samuel* London: Cambridge University Press, 1913), p. 60.

[6] See: Kirkpatrick, p. 1, iii; Hertzberg, pp. 111, 115, 132; Oesterley, pp. 71-72; Julius Wellhausen, *Prolegomena to the History of Israel,* trans. J. Sutherland Black and Allan Menzies (Edinburgh: Adam and Charles Black, 1895), p. 450; P. Kyle McCarter, Jr., *I Samuel: A New Translation with Introduction, Notes, and Commentary* (Garden City, New York: Doubleday, 1980) 251; S.R. Driver, *Notes on the Hebrew Text and the Topography of the Books of Samuel with an Introduction in Hebrew Palaeography and the Ancient Versions* (Oxford: Clarendon, 1913), pp. 114-115; Joseph Blenkinsopp, "Jonathan's Sacrilege: I SM 14, 1-46: A Study in Literary History," *Catholic Biblical Quarterly* 26 (1964), pp. 444-445; and Bruce C. Birch, Society of Biblical Literature Dissertation Series 27 (Missoula, Montana: Scholars Press, 1976), p. 125 n. 151.

[7] Kirkpatrick, p. 1 iii. Blenkinsopp, pp. 444-445, observes that "I SM 14 is an incident in the Philistine war, a war which must be considered a bridge between the old order or a loose tribal confederation and the new ostensibly secular reality of the monarchy."

[8] McCarter, pp. 248-251, says: (1) that "nowhere in the OT is such detail given concerning casting lots," and (2) that the prophetic author of 1 Samuel 13:7b-15a selected the accounts of the battle of Michmash Pass and the cursing of Jonathan because they showed what the author believed to be true about Saul, i.e., that he tried to manipulate the divine will through ritual formality. See, also: Ackroyd, pp. 112-114; and Kirkpatrick, p. 96.

[9] The term used in eye-brightening episode, **tāro' enāh 'enāw**, in other biblical passages [e.g., Ps 13:4 (MT 3) and Ezra 9:8] involves God's participation and may suggest the same here.

[10] Kirkpatrick, p. 96.

[11] Jobling (1976), pp. 369-370.

[12] Ackroyd (1971), pp. 112, 115.

[13] Hertzberg, p. 244. Blenkinsopp, pp.427-431, finds within 1 Samuel 14 the thematic, theological and literary Holy War pattern similar to the narratives of the period of the judges and notes, also, that the supernatural panic of 1 Sam 14 is short of desirable. Just as Jonathan the hero is not so heroic, the battle itself accomplishes little, and even puts Israel at a disadvantage. Also, in

making a connection with J material in Genesis, e.g., The eating of honey with the eating of forbidden fruit, Blenkinsopp does not acknowledge that the outcomes differ. Jonathan is not punished, nor is his increased seeing, "eyes brightened," negative. The "familiar" formulae and structures receive not so subtle twists. The Holy Way accomplishes little, and the rebellious Jonathan is not taken down a peg or two as Adam and Eve.

Notice that David's subsequent fight with Goliath, also an individualistic and unconventional bout, is not fraught with Holy Way formula and priestly intrigue, and yet the consequences are enormously positive, both immediately (1 Sam 17:52) and in the longer run (1 Sam 18:6) in terms of David's development as a leader and in terms of Israel's military position. Genre differences are probably a factor here in the different accounts of Jonathan and David as warriors--the Jonathan accounts being more annalistic, and the David-Goliath account more legendary or saga-like.

[14] Jobling (1976), p. 372ff.

[15] J. A. Thompson, "The Significance of the Verb Love in the David-Jonathan Narratives in 1 Samuel, "Vetus Testamentum 24 (1974), p. 334. He then lists six references to covenants in 1 and 2 Samuel--one does not involve David at all, two are the Jonathan-David covenant, and two others refer to the same covenant with Abner.

[16] The eleven occurrences are as follows: 1 Sam 11:1-2, Nabash and men of Jabesh make a treaty; 1 Sam 18:3, Jonathan and David make a covenant; 1 Sam 20:8, Reference to David-Jonathan covenant as "sacred covenant" (RSV), "covenant of Yahweh" (MT); 1 Sam 20:16, Greek MT has "and Jonathan made a covenant with the house of David;" possibly 1 Sam 20:30, Saul accuses and insults Jonathan for choosing [entering into covenant with; qal pt. of **bāḥar**] the son of Jesse; 1 Sam 22:8, Saul says, "My son makes a league [**kārat**] with the son of Jesse;" 1 Sam 23:18, Jonathan and David make a covenant before Yahweh; 2 Sam 3:12-13, 21, David makes a covenant with Abner (plans to make one with Israel); 2 Sam 5:3, David makes a covenant with the Elders of Israel; 2 Sam 21:7, Reference to the "oath [**sebuʿat**] of Yahweh between. . . . David and Jonathan;" and 2 Sam 23:5, Reference to God's "everlasting covenant" with David.

[17] See Jobling (1978), p. 6; and Kirkpatrick, p.436. Driver, pp. 359-360, makes a case for the covenant-nature of 2 Samuel 7:12 ff. by reason of the forensic language used.

[18] Jobling (1978), p. 19, 13-14, states that "no one is ever representee as assuming other [than that the kingship passes through a male line]." See, also: Gunn (1980), pp. 14, 80, 81, 84, 93, 120; and Ackroyd (1971), pp. 147, 167.

[19] Jonathan comments about David's kingship twice (1 Sam 20:12-17 and 23:23:15-18). In the former Jonathan implies and wishes for David to be king; in the latter he states as a fact that David will be king. In neither does he mention a Davidic dynasty. The explicit statement involves no mention of descendants and houses. Although the implicit statement talks of protection of his house, his remark in 1 Sam 20:14, "If I am still alive," could well mean that he will need protection from his angry father and not from David (i.e., according to the oriental custom of of the new king's killing off the old king's family--Kirkpatrick, p. 168). But even the need for protection from David's house would not necessarily mean that David would establish a dynasty. From what Jonathan says we could more easily interpret his remarks as supporting matrilineal kingship--David's marriage to Michal--than violating patrilineal kingship.

[20] See, also, **mamelākâ**, "kingdom," used in 1 Sam 13:13; 15:28 and 28:17.

[21] For comprehensive listing of Saul's sons compiled from various passages, see Ackroyd (1971), p. 227. Following from 1 Sam 9:20, where Samuel says to Saul, "And for whom is all that is desirable in Israel? Is it not for you and all your father's house?," Pedersen, I-II, p. 269, maintains that "every member of Saul's family had in himself an inborn claim to share in the glory of rulership." Although he does not elaborate as to wether such "sharing" meant direct access to the throne, we are reminded that a first son's abdication would not necessarily remove the kingship from the house, but would pass it to the next son.

[22] See, for example: Gunn (1980), p. 80; Ackroyd (1971), p. 147; Oesterley, p. 93; S. Goldman, Samuel, *Hebrew Text and English Translation with an Introduction and Commentary* (London: Soncino Press, 1951) p. 110; and William McKane, *I and II Samuel: Introduction and Commentary* (London: SCM, 1963) p. 115. Gunn supports his reading of a transfer of royalty via clothing with 1 Sam 15:27-28; here Samuel's robe is torn by Saul and Samuel responds by saying that "Yahweh has torn the kingdom of Israel from you this day, and has given it to a neighbor of yours" (cf., 1 Sam 24:11). A major difference, however, is that Saul has a kingdom to tear; Jonathan does not.

[23] Goldman, p. 110.

[24] Oesterley, p. 93; and McKane, p. 115, add that **pāsaṭ**, "to strip," relates to the ancient semitic belief that a person's clothes were part of oneself and that be giving his clothes to David, Jonathan and David became one flesh. According to William Roberson Smith, *Lectures on the Religion of the Semites* (London: A & C Black, 1927) p. 235, giving part of oneself through an offering of clothes in the Arab world was a means by which others could bear witness to an agreement or covenant and by which the agreement had a future physical manifestation. The item worn, therefore, had to be an item that would always be worn, and frequently among Arabs was a simple knot tied in the other's headshawl. Pedersen, I-II, p. 269, elaborates further on the gift-giving aspect of covenant-making as a means of solidifying an agreement.

[25] Jobling (1978), p. 13.

[26] Also, in 1 Sam 19:6, Saul says **ḥay-yehwâh**, "as Yahweh lives," not **ḥolîlâ**, "far from it."

[27] Kirkpatrick, p. 173. Ackroyd (1971), p. 168, also, finds David's behavior an "appropriate gesture before the king's son."

[28] Furthermore, the term is used variously in other places in 1 and 2 Samuel. In 1 Sam 17:41 it describes physical location, not status. Used specifically with David, it has him coming "before the people" in 1 Sam 18:16. And Saul is himself in awe "before David" in 1 Sam 18:15.

[29] Jonathan's saying in 1 Sam 23:17 that he would be **misneh** does not mean that David is replacing him. To be David's "second-in-command" (McCarter, p. 372) does not mean that he thinks of himself as moving down. Other translations minimize even more any presumed inequality of substitution, e.g., "next to you" (RSV), "next unto thee" (Kirkpatrick, p. 188), or my own "I shall be your double."

[30] The image of Ishbaal's being killed in his sleep (2 Sam 4:7) is not that of an aspiring ruler, especially when contrasted with David's escape from nighttime attempts on his life (1 Sam 19:12).

[31] Rost, however, as cited by David M. Gunn, *The Story of King David: Genre and Interpretation,* Journal for the Study of the Old Testament Supplement Series 6 (Sheffield, England: JSOT Press, 1978; reprint ed., 1982) p. 68, suggests that the introductory inquiry of 2 Sam 9:1 ("Is there still anyone left of the house of Saul?") presupposes the story of the Gibeonites' revenge (2 Samuel 21).

[32] Gunn (1982), p. 82, says that the Meribbaal sub-plot comes into focus as "succession" material allowing an interpretation of the theme of David's succession to slide from one distinct understanding of one theme ("Which son shall rule?") to another ("Will David establish a dynasty at all?"). The tension is not around Solomon succession, but around succession at all. Gunn's interpretation would underscore that patrilineal rule is either not assumed by the narrative or presented as historically not in place at the time of the story's events.

[33] *The New Oxford Annotated Bible with Apocrypha*, Revised Standard Version, p. 386; see also, Gunn (1982), pp. 68-70.

[34] Another factor making Merribbaal's claim and aspirations to the throne a moot point is his lameness, since such a condition would probably eliminate him from ever being a king (cf. 1 Sam 9:2; 16:12, 2 Sam 14:25); see Arvid S. Kapelrud, "King David and the Sons of Saul, " *The Sacral Kingship: Contributions to the Central Theme of the VIIIth International Congress for the History of Religion* (Rome, April 1955) in Studies in the History of Religions (Supplement to "Numen") (Leiden, The Netherlands, 1959) vol. IV, pp. 297-298.

[35] Thompson, pp. 336-337. His argument for a political as well as a personal meaning, or for a personal expression to serve as a vehicle for political alliance, is not far-fetched. William L. Moran, "The Ancient Near Eastern Background of the Love of God in Deuteronomy," *Catholic Biblical Quarterly* 25 (1963), p. 80, shows that "coming down to the first millenium, we find this terminology still in use. . . . A vassal must love his sovereign. . . . 'You will love as yourselves Assurbanipal.'"

[36] Notice that in Lev 19:18, another term, **kemô**, "just as" is used with **re'a,** as it is with **ger**, "sojourner" in Lev 19:34.

[37] See Peter R. Ackroyd, "The Verb Love--**'aheb** in the David Jonathan Narratives--A Footnote," *Vetus Testamentum* 25 (1975), p. 213.

[38] Driver, p. 149; and Walter Harrelson, *Interpreting the Old Testament* (New York: Holt, Rinehart and Winston, 1964), p.168.

[39] See McKane, p. 137; and A. R. S. Kennedy, Samuel, *The New Century Bible* (Edinburgh: T. C. and E. C. Jack, [n.d.]; New York: Henry Frowde, [n.d.]), p. 151.

[40] Ackroyd (1971), p. 231.

[41] John L. McKenzie, "The Four Samuels," *Biblical Research* 7 (1962), p. 12.

[42] Gunn (1980), p. 126.

[43] Kennedy, p. 197.

[44] Driver, p. 239.

[45] Moran, pp. 81-82.

[46] Gunn (1980), p. 84.

[47] Jobling (1978), p. 20.

[48] Hertzberg, p. 138.

[49] Goldman, p. 284.

[50] Gunn (1982), p. 138.

[51] Joseph Cady, "'Drum Taps' and Nineteenth-Century Male Homosexual Literature," in *Walt Whitman: Here and Now*, ed. J. P. Krieg (Westport, Connecticut: Greenwood, 1985), p. 52.

[52] Cady, p. 53.

[53] A measure of the success of such coding may be the clarity with which gay persons today tend to read the David-Jonathan relationship as romantic and non-gay persons as political or friendly. Compare, for example, Tom Horner, *Jonathan Loved David: Homosexuality in Biblical Times* (Philadelphia: Westminster, 1978); and John Boswell, *Christianity, Social Tolerance, and Homosexuality: Gay People in Western Europe from the Beginning of the Christian Era to the Fourteenth Century* (Chicago: University of Chicago Press, 1980), pp. 238-239, 252; with Gerald T. Sheppard, "The Use of Scripture within the Christian Ethical Debate Concerning Same-Sex Orientated Persons," *USQR* 40 (1985), pp. 21, 34 n. 27; Derrick Sherwin Bailey, *Homosexuality and the Western Christian Tradition* (London: Longmans, Green, 1955), pp. 56-57; Kirkpatrick, p. 152; and *The Universal Jewish Encyclopedia*, pp. 6, 180. However, note the omission or avoidance of any discussion of Jonathan and David's relationship by non-gay scholar George R. Edwards, *Gay/Lesbian Liberation: A Biblical Perspective* (New York: Pilgrim, 1984) and by gay scholar John J. McNeill, *The Church and the Homosexual* (Kansas City, Kansas: Sheed Andrews and McMeel, 1976).

[54] See for example, Tennyson's *In Memoriam* and Whitman's "Vigil Strange I Kept on the Field One Night" from *Drum-Taps*..

[55] Perhaps, though, the coding was not subtle enough since the Vulgate has: "As a mother loveth her only son, so did I love thee" (Kirkpatrick, p. 250).

[56] I find encouragement in Adrienne Rich's advice about recovering and re-claiming our past: "We need a lot more documentation about what actually happened. I think we can also imagine it, because we know it happened--we know it out of our own lives" (Adrienne Rich in Elly Bulkin, "An Interview with Adrienne Rich: Part I," *Conditions: One* 1 (April 1977), p. 62).

IV. Jeffrey J. Kripal

Ramakrishna's Foot: Mystical Homoeroticism in the *Kathāmṛta*

Ramakrishna was a nineteenth-century Bengali mystic whose life, visions, mystical experiences, and teachings have come down to us in two major Bengali texts: Mahendranath Gupta's *Śrīśrīrāmakṛṣṇakathāmṛta*,[1] known to Bengalis simply as the *Kathāmṛta* and to English readers as *The Gospel of Sri Ramakrishna*,[2] and Swami Saradananda's *Śrīśrīrāmakṛṣṇalīlāprasaṅga*,[3] a hagio-biographical piece known in English under the title *The Great Master*.[4] Gupta's *Kathāmṛta*, which will be the main focus of my comments, records in five volumes (1902, 1904, 1908, 1910, 1932) the conversations Ramakrishna had with his disciples from 1882, the year Gupta met Ramakrishna, to the year of the saint's death in 1886. What is curious about these five volumes is the fact that they are arranged cyclically, that is, instead of a linear chronological sequence (volume one starting with 1882, and volume five ending in 1886), we find that each volume begins anew with 1882 and ends again in 1886. As we have demonstrated elsewhere,[5] the volumes are so structured in order to conceal, however intentionally, a secret. The best way to demonstrate this is to analyze Ramakrishna's "secret talk" (*guhya kathā*)—twenty passages dealing with visions and confessions Ramakrishna thought too troubling or important to reveal to any but his most intimate disciples, what he called his "inner circle" (*antaraṅga*)—and its distribution throughout the five volumes. What we find is that this "secret talk" is held back in volume one (there is not a single occurrence), hinted at in volume two (the term is used once in a section heading), toyed with in volume three (there are six, relatively innocuous, occurrences), and finally revealed in volumes four and five (with thirteen, often potentially scandalous, occurrences between them). What we have, then, is a text structured around an attempt to present certain, more culturally acceptable, aspects of Ramakrishna "up front," and to push the more "secret" dimensions of Ramakrishna into the background.

But Gupta, whose very name means "the hidden"[6] and who preferred to hide even "the hidden" and be called simply "M," *did* reveal the contents of Ramakrishna's secret talk, if only in volumes four (1910) and five (1932).[7] In his English translation, *The Gospel of Sri Ramakrishna*, Nikhilananda, on the other hand, systematically concealed the secret M had reluctantly revealed. Nikhilananda violated both the form and the content of M's *Kathāmṛta*, arranging the scenes in a neat linear sequence and ingeniously mistranslating many of the secrets; those passages for which he could not find a suitably safe enough "translation," he simply omitted. Nikhilananda's claim, then, that "I have made a literal translation, omitting only a few pages of no particular interest to English-speaking readers"[8] should not be taken seriously. Those "few pages of no particular interest" contain some of the most revealing passages of the entire text.

The present essay was conceived as part of a larger project that attempts to reveal and interpret Ramakrishna's secret.[9] The basic thesis of the project and this paper is that Ramakrishna's mystical experiences were driven by erotic energies that he neither fully accepted nor understood. Ramakrishna's secret is a Tantric secret—human sexuality and (at least, Ramakrishna's) mystical experience are joined at the hips. Ramakrishna, who was quite conversant though very uncomfortable with Tantra, often questioned or even denied this connection between sexuality and mystical experience. In other words, *Ramakrishna's secret was secret even to himself.* This becomes particularly clear when we see how Ramakrishna, puzzled by his own visions and behavior, consistently turned to others for commentary, explanation, and defense in the face of criticism. Ramakrishna's secret, then, has been doubly concealed: from the mystic himself in visionary symbolism and unconscious ecstatic acts, and from us in M's five cyclical volumes and Nikhilananda's bowdlerized translation. We thus first need to reject Nikhilananda's translation and go back to the original Bengali text. But this is not enough. Even once we have Ramakrishna's "secret talk" in its literalness, we still have not revealed Ramakrishna's secret. We also need a way to read Ramakrishna's visions, bodily gestures, and mystical experiences as portrayed in the text, for they do not speak of themselves. We must interpret.

The hermeneutical task begins with a problem: Ramakrishna's words often seem to contradict our basic thesis. For example, when a disciple mouthed the Tantric dictum that "The same mystical energy (*śakti*) that results in the bliss of God also produces the pleasure of sensual experience," Ramakrishna retorted: "What is this? Can the power that produces children be the same power that results in the experience of God?"[10] To get around this initial challenge, we will begin by turning to the mystic's body, and more specifically, to his foot: often when Ramakrishna would go into *samādhi* ("ecstasy"), he would place his foot in the "pure" lap of a male disciple. When scandalized observers would confront him after he had emerged from *samādhi*, Ramakrishna would defend himself by insisting that he had no control over his actions while he was in ecstasy. He neither denied the action nor attempted to interpret its meaning; he simply refused to acknowledge it as his own. We disagree with Ramakrishna. We agree with Ramakrishna's foot. Or more precisely, we disagree with Ramakrishna's understanding of the relationship between the sexual and the mystical. We agree with *our interpretation of* Ramakrishna's foot. As with Ramakrishna's "secret talk," Ramakrishna's foot does not speak of itself. It is just a foot, oddly placed perhaps, but still just a foot, recorded in a particular text. As such, it needs to be understood in a larger religious and cultural world. It needs to be located in a particular text filled with other occurrences and metaphors that might suggest to us different aspects of its meaning. In short, *it needs to be interpreted.* In what sense it is a symbol of the mystico-erotic base of one type of religious experience needs to be defined and defended. So let us proceed to Ramakrishna's foot and to the "secrets" of the *Kathāmṛta* with which we will decipher its meaning.

1. Ramakrishna's Foot

Feet are the sacred meeting point of the human and the divine in Indian culture. That which is lowest on the body of the guru or of God is the very highest that humanity, caught in its sufferings and delusions, can ever hope to reach: at the sacred feet, the highest of the low may touch the lowest of the high. Consequently, common forms of homage to one's guru include drinking the water with which his feet have been washed or placing one's head (the highest part of one's body) on his feet (the lowest part of his). Related to this symbolism of the low and the high on the human body is the fact that feet also represent that which is most humble, even that which is despised. As early as the *Ṛg Veda* in the famous "Hymn of Man" (10.90), the four classes (*varṇa*) of Indian society are created when Puruṣa, the Cosmic Man, is sacrificed and dismembered: his mouth becomes the sacred priest, his arms the mighty warrior, his thighs the people, and his feet the lowly servant.[11] Feet, then, are associated with lowliness but also with grace, the guru's grace and God's grace.

We see these connotations worked out in the *Kathāmṛta*. Feet are lowly. Ramakrishna describes himself as "the dust of the dust of the devotee's feet."[12] Disciples take the dust of one another's feet as a sign of humility or of intellectual defeat after an argument.[13] Feet establish social and spiritual hierarchy. Narendra tells his brother disciples that they are of the "servant class" and brags that they all will rub his feet some day. "Go get me a smoke," he commands them. The brothers laugh.[14] Feet are used as instruments of ridicule: Chandra Haldar, convinced that Ramakrishna's ecstasies are a sham and jealous of the saint's ability to charm the temple officer, kicks the ecstatic Ramakrishna with his boots.[15] Along the same lines, feet, especially booted ones, are symbols of colonial oppression and economic domination: Ramakrishna explains to his male devotees that they work "under the Englishman's boots" because their wives henpeck them for this and that luxury. In a baffling display of misogyny, Ramakrishna manages to blame Bengali women for, among all things, colonialism.[16] Feet are feminine and masculine. Drawing on a culturally widespread opposition between the left and the right as the feminine and the masculine, Ramakrishna is said to place his left foot first when walking, just like a woman.[17] Feet are places of contact between the divine and the human. "The lotus feet of God" is a phrase that occurs numerous times in the *Kathāmṛta*.[18] Ramakrishna sings songs to Kālī's black feet, stained with blood, yet as beautiful as a lotus surrounded by bees buzzing in delight.[19] In another song, the lover of God is encouraged to meditate on the Lord's feet "in the lotus seat of the heart."[20] Feet are also places of contact between the guru and the disciple. To massage the guru's feet, for example, is a common act of homage. It was a service Ramakrishna often asked of his (always male) disciples.[21] Again, the guru's feet, like God's feet, are the place of contact between the divine and the human. An ecstatic smiling Ramakrishna places his foot in a scholar's lap and then on his chest, after which the scholar grabs Ramakrishna's foot and prays for spiritual awakening.[22] But not everyone is allowed such contact. The superstitious Kedar stubbornly holds onto Ramakrishna's big toe with the hope of receiving magical powers (*śakti*), annoying Ramakrishna and moving him to pray to Kālī: "Mā, get him out of here!"[23] Women especially are prevented from touching Ramakrishna's feet. A maidservant innocently touches Ramakrishna's feet in a common gesture of homage only to find the saint shouting in protest, panting in terror, and running for Ganges water to purify his now defiled toes.[24]

But most significant for our purposes, feet, at least Ramakrishna's feet, are mystical organs through which Ramakrishna transmits his spiritual powers and energies (*śakti*) to his disciples. Upon first meeting Narendra, who would later become Swami Vivekananda, Ramakrishna placed his right foot[25] on Narendra's chest and sent him, despite Narendra's vociferous protests, into a dizzying mystical experience. The erotic nature of such an act becomes a bit clearer when, years later, seeing Narendra stretched out on the floor, Ramakrishna touches Narendra's knee with his foot and immediately goes into *samādhi*.[26] Songs are sung, and Ramakrishna falls into ecstasy again. Eventually, Ramakrishna comes back to normal consciousness, sits down with his disciples, and tells them that, "He [Narendra] has a man's nature. I have a woman's nature."[27] In another context, Ramakrishna sees flames streaming from Tarak's body as the boy walks away. When he returns a few days later, Ramakrishna describes how "in ecstasy He who is within this [pointing to his own body] put my foot on his chest."[28] Similarly, Bijoy exclaims to Ramakrishna. "I know who you are!" and then takes Ramakrishna's foot and places it on his own chest, whereupon Ramakrishna goes into ecstasy.[29] Here we move beyond the guru's feet to suggestions of something more, to the possibility of interpreting Ramakrishna's foot as the foot of God and Ramakrishna himself as an *avatāra*, a "descent" or incarnation of God.

This becomes explicit in a particular revealing section in which Dr. Sarkar, who was at the time treating Ramakrishna for the throat cancer that would eventually take the saint's life, argues with Girish Ghosh, the famous playwright and devout disciple of Ramakrishna, about the meaning of Ramakrishna's foot:[30]

> Doctor Sarkar: "Well, when you go into ecstasy (*bhāva*), you place your foot on peoples' bodies.[31] This is not good."
> Sri Ramakrishna: "I cannot tell whether or not I place my foot on anyone's body!"
> Doctor Sarkar: "That is not good. Don't you feel this, just a little?"
> Sri Ramakrishna: "What happens to me in that state of ecstasy, can I explain this to you? After such a state I have thought that perhaps this is why I am ill now. In order to experience God I have become mad (*unmāda*). When I enter such a maddened state, what can I do?"
> Doctor Sarkar: "He admits it. He expresses regret for what he does. He is aware that this act is 'sinful' [English word used]."
> Sri Ramakrishna (to Narendra): "You're very bright. Why don't you say something? Why don't you explain it to him?"
> Girish (to Dr. Sarkar): "My good sir! You are mistaken. He has not become ill on account of this. His body is pure, without sin. He touches people for

> their own good. Taking their sin upon himself, he has become ill, such is his thought from time to time..."
> Doctor Sarkar (becoming embarassed, to Girish): "I have been defeated by you. Give me the dust of your feet." (He takes the dust of Girish's feet.)

Dr. Sarkar suggests that Ramakrishna believes he is ill because of his "sinful" acts. Ramakrishna, not at all sure why he does such things and quite unable to defend himself, turns to his beloved Narendra for help. But the ever-fiery Girish steps in and insists that Ramakrishna is sick because he has vicariously absorbed *other* people's sins.[32] Dr. Sarkar admits defeat. But the argument is not over. Dr. Sarkar will insist again and again that the devotees are spoiling Ramakrishna by taking the dust of his feet and filling his head with the idea that he is an incarnation. Such actions can only produce egotism (*ahaṁkāra*) in an otherwise positively delightful soul.[33] For Sarkar, a foot is a foot and a man is a man. To prove his point, Sarkar takes the dust of everyone's feet. But the devotees are not convinced. M speculates: "Is he [Ramakrishna] another incarnation? Is this why people take the dust of his feet?"[34] Whatever the reason, it was Ramakrishna who had the last word in the matter, or perhaps better, the last act: Ramakrishna fell into ecstasy and placed his foot in Dr. Sarkar's lap, explaining to the doctor upon his return, "You are very pure! Otherwise I would not be able to place my foot there!"[35]

So we see a whole range of opinions focused on Ramakrishna's foot. Dr. Sarkar considers Ramakrishna's habit of touching people with his foot while in ecstasy to be "sinful." Girish, employing a strangely Christian model of transference and vicarious suffering,[36] believes that Ramakrishna touches people in order to take their sins upon himself. Kedar, a much more practical man, looks on Ramakrishna's foot as a dispenser of magical powers. Ramakrishna's foot: Sinful? The foot of God? A magical wand? The debate, which we are here entering, was a real one.

2. Anxious Longing and the First Vision

To begin our own look at Ramakrishna's foot, we need to go back to the mystic's first full- blown mystical experience at the age of twenty. The classical account of it, cited extensively and usually assumed to be the only version, occursing Saradananda's *Śrīśrīrāmakṛṣṇalī-lāprasaṅga*. Ramakrishna's elder brother, Ramkumar, who treated Ramakrishna "like a father," has just died, leaving Ramakrishna quite alone. "Who can say to what extent this happening, by driving home the suffering arising from the impermanence of this world, enkindled in his pure mind the fire of renunciation?" Saradananda asks.[37] In any case, it was at this time that Ramakrishna turned to Kālī, the Divine Mother, and sought her vision (*darśana*). Tormented by desire but frustrated by his unsuccessful attempts and at the point of despair, Ramakrishna's eyes fall on the sacrificial sword hanging on the temple wall. The young man reaches for it and is about to decapitate[38] himself before Kālī when the Goddess intervenes:[39]

> It was as if the room, the door, the temple itself, everything vanished—as if there was nothing anywhere! And what I was seeing was a boundless, infinite, conscious ocean of light! Wherever and however far I looked, from all four directions its brilliant rows of waves were thundering towards me with great speed, ready to devour me. And as I watched, the waves fell upon me and all at once pushed me to the bottom. Gasping and thrashing, I fell unconscious!

As this experience was the culmination of Ramakrishna's initial search for Kālī and represented the beginning of his mystical life, the story is absolutely central to all the classical accounts of Ramakrishna's life. What the commentators have failed to note is that the account bears all the linguistic sophistication and interpretive glosses of the learned Saradananda and almost none of the simple "village talk" (*grāmya bhāṣya*)[40] of Ramakrishna, so impressively preserved, if only erratically, in the *Kathāmṛta*. But what we will focus our attention on here is not the rhetoric of the account but the term Ramakrishna used to describe his mental state at the time the experience occurred: *vyākulatā*, "anxious longing," a desire that torments. The word sums up Ramakrishna's feeling at this time and in fact forms the title of the chapter in which Saradananda's classical account occurs: "Anxious Longing and the First Vision" (*Vyākulatā o Prathama Darśana*). Ramakrishna would later elevate the term to a central place in his teaching, where it became an almost technical word for the state of desire necessary before one's mystical yearnings can burst into vision and actual experience. *Vyākulatā*, Ramakrishna taught, is like the purple and red rays of dawn ushering in the morning light of the experience of God. Such desire, Ramakrishna insisted, is absolutely crucial if one is to succeed in the mystical quest. Indeed, if we are to take the dawn-sunrise metaphor seriously, it would seem that such desire *is* the beginning of mystical experience.

A closer look at this purple and crimson desire is revealing. Ramakrishna is portrayed traditionally (and correctly) as likening this "anxious longing" to the gasping urgency one feels when someone holds one's head under the water for too long.[41] So must one feel about seeing God. But so also does Ramakrishna feel about seeing, feeding, and bathing his boy disciples. Ramakrishna describes how, after seeing Narendra for the first time, his "anxious longing" to see Narendra again increased so much that he could hardly breathe. Troubled by the experience, he asks another (much older) disciple why he feels this way for such a boy. The disciple replies that in the *Mahābhārata* it is said that, after emerging from *samādhi* a pure soul can stand only the company of other pure souls, for they alone can calm his spiritualized soul. Hearing this, Ramakrishna's mind was eased a bit, but he continued, nevertheless, to cry for Narendra.[42] Again, troubled by his desire for the boys, Ramakrishna asks M, "Why do I feel so anxious (*vyākulatā*) for them?" M can give no answer before an upset Ramakrishna breaks in, "Why don't you say something?"[43] Similarly, M tells us that Ramakrishna is so anxious (*vyākula*) to see his "inner circle" of disciples that he cannot sleep at night. Instead, he prays to Kālī, "Mā, their love is great. Drag them here. O Mā, bring them here."[44] Ramakrishna loves Naran, a boy of seventeen or eighteeen, a great deal. He sits down and cries, so anxious (*vyākula*) is he to see and feed him.[45] *Vyākulatā*, then, can refer equally well to both mystical longing and Ramakrishna's desire to interact with his male disciples. The two meanings, at least linguistically, are very much related.

With this in mind, let us now turn to a possible textual variant of Ramakrishna's "anxious longing and first vision," this time in the *Kathāmṛta*, and see what it might reveal to us when placed beside our study of *vyākulatā*. Ramakrishna is talking to his disciples about how he conquered lust (*kāma*): "Even in my case, after six months I felt a strange sensation in the breast. Then sitting beneath the tree I began to cry. I said, 'O Mā! If this continues, then I shall cut my throat with a knife!'"[46] The passage is much less ornate than Saradananda's account of Ramakrishna's attempted suicide but may hint at a "secret" dimension to Ramakrishna's "anxious longing and first vision" not at all apparent in Saradananda's more classical account of the same event. Let us pursue the textual strands of the passage and their place in the warp and woof of the text and see if we can detect any patterns.

From the context of the passage, we can safely conclude that Ramakrishna's "strange sensation" had something to do with some form of sexual desire, with "lust," but that is about all we can say. As both passages are formed around a threatened self-decapitation, we have speculated that the passage is a variant of the famous "first vision" scene recorded in the *Līlāprasaṅga* and so refers to the early years of Ramakrishna's *sādhana*.. But the precise nature of the "strange sensation" that led him to threaten suicide is still not clear. The fact that the expression "a strange sensation in the breast" (*buka ki kare*) is used more commonly by women than by men suggests much, but proves little.[47] However, when we find a variant of the same phrase used again in the text, the nature of Ramakrishna's early temptation becomes a bit more clear. Ramakrishna's early erotic crisis is now some twenty years behind him. Now in his late forties, he is talking to M about Purna, a boy of fourteen or fifteen who, as we will see later, figures prominently in Ramakrishna's secret talk and visions:[48]

> Sri Ramakrishna: "If I see Purna one more time, then my anxious longing (*vyākulatā*) might lessen!

> How intelligent he is! He feels a very great attraction for me. He says, 'I also feel a strange sensation (*buka kaemana kare*) to see you.' (to M) They have taken him from your school. Will this cause you trouble?"

Purna and Ramakrishna confess that they feel "a strange sensation" for one another. For a similar feeling years before, Ramakrishna had threatened to cut his throat, and almost succeeded. Now he seems to be quite comfortable with the feeling, which he relates to his "anxious longing" (*vyākulatā*) for the boy Purna. But even here, the nature of this "anxious longing" and "strange sensation" is still not fully revealed. We are told that it has resulted in a situation that might cause M, the schoolteacher, trouble at school, but that is all. Similarly, other passages tease us with what they don't say and leave us reading between the lines. In one passage, for example, M tells us that Ramakrishna was so anxious (*vyākula*) to see Purna that he showed up at M's house late one night and asked M to fetch the boy, which M did.[49] Again, a stray comment that Ramakrishna did not visit Purna at his home is explained a bit later when M tells us that Purna was afraid to visit Ramakrishna lest the saint praise him in public and his relatives hear, for Purna's family objected to him visiting Ramakrishna. In another scene, M gets nervous when Purna scoots closer to Ramakrishna—will others notice?[50]

In the end, the nature of Ramakrishna's love for Purna becomes evident only when we turn to another passage, again in M's *Kathāmṛta*, that record of secrets, where Ramakrishna reveals the secret dimension of his "anxious longing" and "strange sensation" for Purna to M. Ramakrishna, M tells us, was talking to him about the boy Purna: "What I'm telling you—all this is not for others to hear—I want to kiss and embrace man (God) as a woman."[51] M, troubled by Ramakrishna's secret, adds in parentheses after the word "man" the gloss "(God)." Nikhilananda adopts the gloss as the meaning of the sentence, completely neglecting the fact that M specifically says that Ramakrishna was talking about Purna. What we had to read between the lines we now have to read in the Bengali, for it is completely concealed in Nikhilananda's English translation beneath Sanskrit abstractions and Nikhilananda's bowdlerizing agenda: "The devotee looking on himself as Prakriti likes to embrace and kiss God, whom he regards as the Purusha."[52]

So Ramakrishna feels a "strange sensation" for Purna, as Purna does for Ramakrishna. Ramakrishna wants to kiss and to embrace Purna as if he were a woman and Purna a man. The ambivalence Ramakrishna once felt about this "strange sensation" is now shared by Purna's family, who object to the boy seeing Ramakrishna. The nature of their mutual "anxious longing" was such that Ramakrishna could not visit Purna at his own home but had to set up *rendez-vous* points at a third-party's house, sometimes late at night. We began by positing a connection between Ramakrishna's "anxious longing" (*vyākulata*) that led to his first experience of Kālī and the "strange sensation" (*buka ki kare*) for which he threatened to cut his throat, as both events were structured around an attempted or threatened suicide. Now we see that this "strange sensation," which Ramakrishna specifically identified as erotic (*kāma*), is connected, at least linguistically, with the "strange sensation" he felt for Purna. All three experiences (the "anxious longing and first vision," the erotic crisis, and his attraction for Purna) are woven together in the texts by two expressions: "anxious longing" (*vyākulatā*) and "a strange sensation in the breast" (*buka ki kare*).

The textual weave becomes even tighter when we analyze yet another expression used by the texts to describe, again, both the state of desire that ushered in the "first vision" and Ramakrishna's longing for his boy disciples—"wrung like a wet towel" (*gāmchā niṅṛāiyā thāka*). The expression is best known as it is used in the *Līlāprasaṅga* to describe the state of desire that preceded Ramakrishna's first vision of Kālī: "It felt like someone was wringing my heart as if it were a wet towel."[53] As with Ramakrishna's "anxious longing" and "strange sensation," the expression reveals its erotic dimensions only when it is used in contexts other than the famous "first vision." In one passage, Ramakrishna describes his great desire to meet his "inner circle" of boy disciples: "An indescribable yearning to see you all would arise in my heart. The pain, like a wet towel being wrung, was so great that I would become all excited and fall down." Ramakrishna wanted to cry and feared he might go mad. He would climb to the roof of the temple house and call out loudly: "Who are you all, my children? Where are you? Come!"[54] In another passage, Ramakrishna describes his desire to see Narendra as he once described his "anxious longing" to see Kālī: "If he should delay a few days, my heart would feel as if it were being wrung like a towel."[55] In yet another place, Ramakrishna, his heart "forcibly wrung like a wet towel," keeps his guests up all night confessing his anguished desire to see Narendra.[56] And again, Ramakrishna confesses that his heart, "wrung like a wet towel," was so tormented with the desire to see Narendra that he used to run to the northern end of the garden to weep for the boy. This went on for six months.[57] As the passages pile up, a pattern is revealed: in every occurrence of the expression "wrung like a wet towel" in the *Līlāprasaṅga* other than the famous "first vision," and probably even there, the phrase refers to Ramakrishna's anxious desire to establish intimate contacts with young males. Like Ramakrishna's "anxious longing" and "strange sensation," then, his heart "wrung like a wet towel" can express both his desire to see God and his longing to interact with his boy disciples. The linguistic pattern is a familiar one.

Let us sum up what we have accomplished so far. We began with Ramakrishna "anxiously longing" to see Kālī in a passage made famous by nearly all of Ramakrishna's biographers. Noting that this "anxious longing" (*vyākulatā*) preceded an attempted suicide, we then turned to another passage, almost never quoted by the biographers, and saw Ramakrishna threatening to cut his throat with a knife for a "strange sensation" he identified as erotic (*kāma*). We speculated that the two passages might refer to the same incident. We then saw that this "strange sensation" was used in other passages to describe Ramakrishna's "anxious" (*vyākula*) feelings for Purna, a boy of fourteen, whom Ramakrishna confessed he wanted to embrace and kiss as an erotic object. We noted that a pattern can be detected in the weave of the texts by tracing the occurences of the two terms, "anxious longing" and "a strange sensation." We then added a third term, "wrung like a wet towel," to complete our triple pattern. We are thus left with three terms, all of which are used to refer both to Ramakrishna's anxious desire for mystical experience and his homoerotic longing to see, even to embrace and kiss, his boy disciples. Though by no means conclusive, the evidence is suggestive.

From the above, we conclude tentatively that Ramakrishna's attempted decapitation, which led to the saint's first full-blown mystical experience, was triggered by homoerotic longings Ramakrishna was at that time rejecting as illegitimate, as "sinful," to use Dr. Sarkar's word: the pattern created by the terms "anxious longing," "a strange sensation," and "wrung like a wet towel" suggests as much, as *all three terms are explicitly connected with Ramakrishna's threatened self-decapitation and all three terms are used to describe Ramakrishna's attraction for his boy disciples.* By employing a culturally meaningful act—offering one's head to Kālī (who, it should be remembered, wears a garland of such heads around her neck and holds a sword and lopped off head in her left hands)—Ramakrishna attempted to end his erotic torment (*vyākulatā*) by symbolically castrating himself, the head being, in the mystical physiology of yoga and Tantra, the ultimate goal of one's semen and so an appropriate symbol for the phallus.[58] Kālī's sword and her garland of heads thus became "personal symbols" for Ramakrishna in the sense that Obeyesekere has defined them, symbols which carry communicable cultural meanings but are properly interpreted only in reference to the deep motivations of a particular life-history, in this case, Ramakrishna's.[59] Ramakrishna's attempted suicide and consequent experience of Kālī, then, can be understood *both* as a genuinely religious experience driven by mystical longing (the culturally accepted interpretation advanced by Saradananda in his *Līlāprasaṅga*) and as a desperate attempt to put an end to his tormenting guilt fueled by homoerotic longing (as hinted at by Ramakrishna himself in the variant recorded in the *Kathāmṛta*). The latter, it seems, somehow triggered the former—*an erotic crisis led to a mystical experience.* Ramakrishna's "anxious longing and first vision," then, have both a public, culturally interpreted, side and a private, personally meaningful, dimension. We need both to understand and to interpret Ramakrishna's "secret."

3. A Dislocated Arm and the Secret Change

July 15, 1885 was a big day for Ramakrishna's "secret talk." On that day Ramakrishna revealed to his disciples how he once saw the *brahmayoni* ("cosmic vagina") lolling under the banyan tree, how he performed many Tantric *sādhanas* under the same tree, and how the Bhairavī, his female Tantric guru, forced him to take the "seat of __,"[60] most likely a reference to "the seat of bliss" (*ānanda āsana*), that is, the Bhairavī's lap mounted in left-handed Tantric ritual.[61] It was also on the same day that Ramakrishna related how he used to laugh a great deal after he would "teasingly fondle the penis" of a *Paramahaṁsa* boy who would emerge from him,[62] and that he "couldn't help but to worship the penises of boys with sandal-paste and flowers,"[63] two confessions which are either seriously mistranslated or omitted completely by Nikhilananda, allegedly because they are "of no interest to English-speakers."

But for our present purposes, yet another "secret" revealed on that day is particularly important. It concerns an especially mysterious incident, Ramakrishna's dislocated arm. The passage reads as follow:[64]

> Now I am telling you something very secret (*atiguhya kathā*)—why I love Purna, Narendra, and all the others so much. I broke my arm while embracing Lord Jagannath in an erotic mood (*madhura bhāva*). Then it was made known to me: "You have taken a body. Now remain in the different moods—the Friend, the Parent, and the rest—in relation to other forms of man.

Here, Ramakrishna is employing a Vaiṣṇava theology whereby the aspirant assumes different "moods" or "states of being" (*bhāva*) in his or her relationship to Kṛṣṇa. Five such moods are commonly listed: the Peaceful (the aspirant contemplates Kṛṣṇa as the Godhead), the Servant (the aspirant looks on Kṛṣṇa as Lord), the Friend (the aspirant becomes a milk-maid friend of Rādhā, Kṛṣṇa's favorite lover), the Parent (the aspirant becomes Yaśoda, Kṛṣṇa's mother, and looks on Kṛṣṇa as the baby Gopala), and the Erotic (the aspirant becomes Rādhā, Kṛṣṇa's lover). The Erotic mood is commonly accepted as the highest, for it alone subsumes all the others. Ramakrishna's secret vision bears this out, for what we see taking place in it is the transformation of an essentially erotic state, the Erotic or "sweet mood" (*madhura bhāva*), into the other moods. What is particularly significant here is the fact that in the Erotic mood Ramakrishna's energies were directed toward the divine, to "Lord Jagannath," whereas the other moods are to be taken on "in relation to other forms of man." From "embracing Lord Jagannath in an erotic mood," Ramakrishna will turn to his disciples as a mother, as a friend, and as a lover. These relationships, all essentially erotic to the extent that they all are transformations of "the sweet mood," take place in the communal incarnation that is Ramakrishna and his disciples, who have incarnated along with Ramakrishna as his intimate "pieces" (*aṁsa*) and "parts" (*kala*). As such, just as the Godhead became two and incarnated as Rādhā and Kṛṣṇa "in order to taste his own sweetness,"[65] so now Ramakrishna and his disciples constitute "the forms of man" in which God can incarnate again and experience his own mystico-erotic bliss (*ānanda*). No longer capable of experiencing God as formless consciousness, Ramakrishna now wants to see, touch, and embrace God as form, and so he receives the command: "You have taken a body. So take pleasure (*ānanda karā*) in the forms of man."[66] So important is this change to Ramakrishna that he leaves the steps he is sitting on and scoots closer to his disciples to reveal this "secret talk" (*guhya kathā*). In another passage, Ramakrishna explains that God plays as man (*manuṣyalīlā*) in the incarnation in order "to taste the juice of experience" (*rasāsvādana karā*). A little of this "juice," sought by the incarnation, manifests itself in every devotee. It can be extracted only by continuous "sucking," like one sucks the honey out of a flower.[67] This, according to M, is the "secret meaning" (*guhya artha*) of the incarnation and his "play as man" (*naralīlā*).[68]

Although Ramakrishna was said to manifest the Peaceful mood after his ecstasies, the three primary moods that he adopted in relation to his disciples were the Parent, the Friend, and the Erotic. All frumpled upon waking, Ramakrishna looks like a mother ready to nurse her child with her exposed breast, a condition which evokes laughter from the disciples.[69] In another passage, Ramakrishna takes a pillow to his breast and nurses it.[70] Taking on the *bhāva* of Yaśoda, he takes the boy Rakhal as Gopala and places Rakhal's head in his lap.[71] Again, Ramakrishna takes Rakhal into his lap "as if he were nursing him."[72] But despite such actions, Ramakrishna resolutely warned his disciples against being tricked by a female aspirant into take on the "Gopala mood" (in which the aspirant becomes the child Kṛṣṇa in relation to a woman as Yaśoda)—such a mood could easily be used as a religious front for other, less respectable, feelings, he told them.[73] Ramakrishna's fears concerning the "Gopala mood" were most likely based on his early experiences as "the child" of his female Tantric guru, the Bhairavī, who, it might be surmised, tried everything, including force, to get the young Ramakrishna into her lap. In any case, what was considered sexually dangerous and so illegitimate for a woman to do, Ramakrishna felt was perfectly appropriate for him to do. And he did it with abandon—caressing, embracing, bathing, feeding, nursing, and laying his boy disciples down as an erotic mother literally ecstatic over her "Gopala."

But Ramakrishna also took on the Friend mood, becoming a maidservant of Kālī or a girlfriend of Rādhā and, it might be added, of numerous women whom he loved to visit in their rooms in order to mimick their movements and conversation. Stories abound of Ramakrishna, dressed as a woman, going completely unnoticed at public festivals, at the temple, even in the women's inner apartment. As a "maidservant of Mā," Ramakrishna once lived with the women of the temple officer's house. He tells us that, just as little boys and girls are not embarassed around one another, nor were they. He even used to sleep with them.[74] All this came easy for Ramakrishna, for as he proclaimed again and again, "I have an effeminate nature (*meyeli svabhāva*)."[75]

Doctrinally speaking, it is considered inappropriate for an aspirant in Bengali Vaiṣṇavism to take on the *bhāva* of Rādhā, for Rādhā alone merits the distinction of being the archetypal lover of Kṛṣṇa. For the "girlfriend" of Rādhā, then, the Erotic mood is more an ideal to be watched (a sort of mystical voyeurism) than an actual state of being to adopt. But Ramakrishna was not an orthodox Vaiṣṇava and so had no qualms about taking on the "sweet mood" of Rādhā, who, unlike the pure and truthful Sītā, Ramakrishna tells us, likes to flirt (*chenālī*).[76] The description was an apt one, for although Ramakrishna was said to have Sītā's smile,[77] it was definitely as the flirtatious Rādhā that he interacted with his boy disciples. Singing songs to Kṛṣṇa, Ramakrishna would stroke Narendra's face and fall into ecstasy. Seeing an English boy leaning up against a tree, seductively "thrice-bent" (*tribhaṅga*) like Kṛṣṇa,[78] Ramakrishna froze into his own ecstatic pose.[79] The phrase, "mad for Kṛṣṇa," occurs almost as many times as the phrase, "mad for Narendra." Both relationships were acted out and legitimated within a distinctively religious framework, the Vaiṣṇava *bhāvas*. For Ramakrishna as Rādhā, his beloved Narendra *was* Kṛṣṇa. As a result, Ramakrishna's love was a love at once mystical and erotic. As with his "anxious longing and first vision," the erotic both triggered and supported the mystical.

4. *The Avatāra's "Play as Man"*

The dislocated arm is something of a mystery. How exactly Ramakrishna broke it while trying to embrace Jagannath is never really explained. M tells us that Ramakrishna dislocated his left hand when he fell over a rail "on his way to the Pine Grove," a euphemism for "on his way to defecate,"[80] but that is all we are told. Whatever happened, it was after the saint dislocated his left hand in an ecstatic state that he received the command to return to what he called God's "play as man" (*naralīlā*).[81] Sometimes, however, Ramakrishna forgot the command to "Remain in the world."[82] On one such occassion, Ramakrishna lost himself in ecstasy and awoke to find that he had broken his teeth in yet another fall, a painful reminder to "Remain in the world."[83]

God, Ramakrishna taught, is manifest in all things, but God is especially "apparent" (*prakāśa*) in human beings.[84] Consequently, Ramakrishna became ecstatic in crowds of people, for in them, Ramakrishna said, "one can see that 'He[85] has become everything.'"[86] But among men, God is more manifest in some than others. Just as water is water, but only some water is appropriate for drinking and washing, so some people are more spiritually fit, more mystically "powerful" (*śakti*) than others—all men are *not* created equal.[87] Boys are particularly luscent bearers of God's light and power, for their breasts have not yet been covered over by the excrement of worldly concerns[88] and that most damaging of worldly realities—a job.[89] Nor have they fallen into the clutches of "woman-and-gold" (*kāminīkañcana*), that abyss from which the best one can hope is to return "sooty," still alive but defiled.[90] Haramohan was a good example of what happened when a boy disciple married. Ramakrishna once "anxiously longed" (*vyākula*) to see Haramohan, but when the boy married, he quit coming as often, and when he did come, he brought his wife along, the two of them sitting together apart from Ramakrishna. Peaved at this new development, Ramakrishna told Haramohan to leave, explaining, "How can my body touch yours?"[91]

It was the boys in particular whom Ramakrishna served, fed, bathed, and caressed as God: "feeding them is to feed Narāyāṇa (a form of the god Viṣṇu)" he told Balaram, whose house often functioned as a rendezvous point or "temple" for Ramakrishna's meetings with his disciples, young and old.[92] "When the Master looked at a boy disciple," M tells us, "he would float in bliss." For example, when a boy of fifteen walked into a theatre box to see Ramakrishna, M tells us that the saint, "floating in bliss," stroked the young boy with his hand and asked him to sit down. When the boy left, Ramakrishna told M that the boy's physical signs were very good and that "if he would have stayed any longer, I would have stood erect."[93] Again, when it came time for the disciples to leave one evening, Ramakrishna turned to the youth Bhavanath and said, "Please don't leave today. When I look at you, I get all excited (*uddīpana*)!"[94] Ramakrishna glances at little Naran and falls into ecstasy, for "in a pure soul he saw Narāyāṇa."[95] Ramakrishna sits in Niranjan's lap, touches Kalipad's chest, strokes his chin, falls into ecstasy, and then places his foot on their chests.[96] The examples could be multiplied well into the dozens.

But one disciple was an especially fit, an especially powerful bearer of Narāyāṇa's presence—Narendra, Ramakrishna's "beloved disciple."[97] Ramakrishna's love for Narendra was legendary. At one of their first meetings, Ramakrishna embarrassed Narendra by giving him all of his attention in a roomful of people: "Can't you talk to someone else?" an embarassed Narendra implored an insistent Ramakrishna. But to no avail: "But I kept on talking," Ramakrishna tells us.[98] At the saint's second meeting with the young student, Ramakrishna exclaimed, "Narāyāṇa, you have incarnated and come for me!"[99] Then he reached out and touched Narendra, sending Narendra into his first mystical experience. This was only the first of a long line of electric touches. The *Kathāmṛta* is liberally peppered with others. Ramakrishna walks into a room and sees Narendra stretched out on the floor. Ramakrishna, "mad for Narendra," loses himself in ecstasy and sits on Narendra's back.[100] Ramakrishna describes Narendra as an "unsheathed sword"[101] and as an "erect cobra."[102] Or Ramakrishna is the aroused snake and Narendra is the snake charmer: Narendra recalls how Ramakrishna once explained to him that "He who is within this [pointing to his own chest] spreads its hood and stands erect like a cobra to hear your songs!"[103] After one such arousing song, Ramakrishna embraces Narendra again and again and exclaims, "You have given me so much bliss today!"[104] Narendra "lights the fire" of Ramakrishna's ecstasies.[105] Ramakrishna sits in Bholanath's garden, holding his host's hand and weeping for Narendra: "I had become crazy to see him."[106] Later he would weep at the news of Narendra's impending marriage: "O Mā! Don't let Narendra sink!"[107] "Looking at Narendra," Ramakrishna tells his disciples, "my mind is dissolved in the Undivided."[108] "It is good he doesn't come often," Ramakrishna notes to another disciple, "otherwise, I would always be unconscious."[109]

Watching Ramakrishna mother Narendra, M asks himself: "Why does he caress the body and feet of Narendra so? Is he serving Narendra as Narāyāṇa? Or is he infusing Narendra with his mystical power (*śakti*)?"[110] Ramakrishna sings of Rādhā "maddened for love of Kṛṣṇa." Narendra sings, and Ramakrishna falls into ecstasy again. This whole scene invokes serious reflection on M's part (most of which is omitted by Nikhilananda). M thinks to himself: "What love! He is crazy for Narendra and cries for Narāyāṇa! He says, 'These and the other boys are Lord Narāyāṇa himself, they have taken a body for me!' . . . He cries to bathe them, to lay them down, and to see them. He runs all over Calcutta to see them. He flatters and pesters people to bring them from Calcutta to him in their carriages. . . . Is this worldly love (*māyika sneha*)? Or is it the pure love of God (*viśuddha iśvaraprema*)?"[111] M tries to answer his own questions concerning Ramakrishna's embarassingly obvious infatuation with Narendra and, in the process, reveals his own awareness of the physical dimension of Ramakrishna's attraction for the young man:[112]

> Looking at Narendra, he forgets the external world and gradually forgets even the embodied Narendra. He forgets "the apparent man" and begins to see "the real man". His mind dissolves in the unbroken Being-Consciousness-Bliss. ... Exclaiming "Narendra! Narendra!" he becomes crazy!

Ramakrishna's love for Narendra lasted until the very end. Only weeks before he died, Ramakrishna called Narendra to his side and in an ecstatic state transmitted his mystical energies to him (*śaktipāta*). Afterwards, Narendra claims, his body was so charged that when he asked another disciple to touch it, the disciple received a palpable shock.[113] Ramakrishna's mystical energies, then, chose erotic channels to the very end. Now finally embodied in the saint's beloved object, Ramakrishna could die.

Related to this transmission of energies is Ramakrishna's famous commission to Narendra to teach, symbolically preserved in a fascinating drawing that has not received enough attention or comment.[114] His throat swollen with cancer, Ramakrishna drew Narendra's bust facing left with a peahen behind it, facing the back of Narendra's head. "Victory to Rādhā, the embodiment of love! Naren will teach. When he goes outside, he will give a shout. Victory to Rādhā!" is written (in poor Bengali) above the drawing. Now the peacock is an erotic symbol in Vaiṣṇava poetry, for its dance ushers in the rainy season, the season for making love. Accordingly, Ramakrishna tells us that when Rādhā sees a dark cloud or the blue neck of a peacock, she is "ecstatically reminded" (*uddīpana*) of her dark blue lover, Kṛṣṇa, and falls down unconscious.[115] But peacocks are also proud teachers for Ramakrishna. The saint described how he saw in a vision the form of his friend, Keshab Sen, before he ever actually met him in person: Keshab appeared in the vision as a proud peacock showing off his colors in order to attract a great following as a teacher of men.[116] With his images and words, then, Ramakrishna seems to be identifying himself both with Rādhā, the lover of Kṛṣṇa, and with the peahen, who arouses the peacock to display for all men its gorgeous feathers. If we continue to unpack the symbolism, we might speculate that Ramakrishna's commission to Narendra to teach was an essentially erotic act, for the peacock's display is intended primarily for its mate (in this case, the feminine Ramakrishna); that it also gives delight to any onlookers seems almost beside the point. But beside the point or not, Narendra's presence and words, like the peacock's display, would indeed be very colorful, a delight for many, just as they had once "lighted the fire" of his peahen, Ramakrishna.

5. *Phallic Love and the Avatāra's Erotic Community*

Ramakrishna described his love for God as *rāgabhakti*, a "passionate love" which, unlike conventional love driven by prescription and duty (*vaidhibhakti*), is spontaneous and deep-rooted, "like Śiva's *liṅgam* that stretches down even to Benares." It is this love, likened to a mystical phallus (*Śiva-liṅgam*), that the *avatāra* shares with his disciples.[117] Awed by the person of Ramakrishna, M asks himself, "Is Sri Ramakrishna an *avatāra*, a *Śiva-liṅgam* thrust straight up from the underworld?"[118] In another place, Ramakrishna spits on rituals and rosaries, comparing himself to a self-born *liṅgam* "thrust straight up from the underworld,"[119] in no need of forced acts and constructed intentions.[120]

Now it has been argued that Śiva's *liṅgam* is not really a phallus at all but an abstract symbol of the Godhead, despite the fact that Śiva does all sorts of phallic things with it. In the Purāṇas, for example, he seduces the forest sages' wives with it and then, when angered by their husbands' protests, cuts it off and sends it crashing to the earth where it burns out of control until the sages promise to worship it. The arguments against a phallic interpretation are usually based on the fact that many modern Hindus are completely unaware of its history and sexual connotations. For them, it is argued, the *liṅgam* is nothing more than a symbol of divinity. Perhaps, but such was certainly not the case for Ramakrishna, who worshipped his own penis "with a pearl"[121] as the "living *lingam*.."[122] Nor would such an argument likely convince the *tāntrika* who one day paid Ramakrishna a visit. The "stem" and "lotus flowers" of *kuṇḍalinī* yoga,[123] the *tāntrika* pointed out, symbolize Śiva's phallus (*lingam*) and the Goddess's vagina (*yonirūpa*) in the act of intercourse.[124] For the *tāntrika*, the latent was manifest. Nikhilananda, however, uncomfortable with such a manifest meaning, chose to omit the *tāntrika*'s interpretation from his translation, effectively converting the manifest back into the latent. The Tantric interpretation was excised from the text. We are back to concealing secrets.

Ramakrishna used various techniques and metaphors to awaken this "passionate love," likened to a symbolic phallus, among his disciples. Singing and dancing were particularly popular. Often, Ramakrishna would dance naked, surrounded by his male disciples,[125] or pace,[126] or sit naked among them.[127] Sometimes the boys would dance naked.[128] For Ramakrishna, nudity was a natural expression of the mystical state: when the *kuṇḍalinī* rises "from the feet to the head," one's garments automatically fall off.[129] Even the brahmin's sacred thread, so small yet representing so much, is blown away in the casteless storm of that "state" (*avasthā*). Answering a devotee who was critical of Ramakrishna's casting off of the sacred thread, Ramakrishna explained: "When this state came upon me, then, as in a great storm, everything was blown away. Nothing of before remained. I was unconscious! When my clothes were falling off, how could I keep the sacred thread?"[130] It was particularly as "the Paramahaṁsa" that Ramakrishna practiced his mystical nudity. M described Ramakrishna in "the state of the Paramahaṁsa" (*paramahaṁser avasthā*) thus: "He moves like a child! He grins again and again! He is wearing nothing around his waist. He is naked. His eyes float in bliss!"[131]

Just as nudity is a naked sign of the mystical state, so it is necessary in order to reveal a man's mystical potential, recorded for the trained eye in the curves, colors, and shapes of the human body. Accordingly, Ramakrishna would ask to examine the bare chests of men and boys in order to determine their spiritual fitness.[132] Sometimes, he would go further: one day, he asked the boy Prasanna to strip for him, whereupon Ramakrishna exclaimed,

"What a boy!"[133] He also tried to pair the disciples up into "masculine" and "feminine" disciples, presumably in order to awaken their devotion and love. Narendra, little Naran, and Purna (who, it might be added, figure most prominently as the objects of Ramakrishna's "feminine" love) all have a "masculine essence" (*puruṣasattā*).[134] Bhaburam, whom Ramakrishna "sees" dressed up like the Goddess, along with Bhavanath, Nityagopal, and Harish all have a "woman's nature" (*prakṛtibhāva*).[135] Harish, for example, sleeps in women's clothes.[136] Ramakrishna points out that whereas the feminine disciples are more likely to undergo the "moods" (*bhāva*) and experience their bodies as flushed, masculine disciples do not experience the moods but tend to become dissolved in the Absolute.[137] Narendra, for example, has a man's nature and so naturally tends to a "very high state," to a formless state.[138] Also, since Narendra's nature is masculine, he sits on the right side of the carriage, whereas Ramakrishna, having a woman' s nature, sits on the left.[139] To encourage such genderizing and the love it awakens, Ramakrishna asked Bhavanath to rent a house near Narendra's, for the two, in Ramakrishna's eyes, were like "man and woman."[140]

Ramakrishna used two fascinating theological models to accomplish similar ends—the notion that he and his disciples constituted what we have called a "communal incarnation" of Caitanya and *his* disciples; and the identification of his disciples with the different "lotuses" of the subtle body. Ramakrishna tells us that when an incarnation descends to earth, his retinue of disciples descends with him. These disciples are of three types: the "inner circle" (*antaraṅga*), the "outer circle" (*bahiraṅga*), and the "providers" (*rasaddāra*).[141] Ramakrishna spoke of particular disciples (those in the "inner circle") as "parts" (*kala*) of him: Purna, for example, was considered such a "part" of Ramakrishna.[142] So much did Ramakrishna love the boy that M speculates whether he might be the last member of the elite "inner circle."[143] It was these "parts," as inseparable elements of the communal incarnation, who have incarnated along with Ramakrishna as his "friends and followers" (*sāṅgopāṅga*). Accordingly, Ramakrishna once saw "with open eyes" Caitanya and his disciples dancing in the temple precincts. Later, when certain disciples finally showed up at the temple, Ramakrishna would "stand up with a start," recognizing them as members of the retinue he had seen in his vision.[144] On another occassion, he exclaimed, "I am Advaita, Caitanya, and Nityananda in one."[145] In a slightly different theological context, Ramakrishna claimed that the boy Rakhal was a reincarnation of one of the cowherd boys that joined the divine Kṛṣṇa in his boyhood pranks and games.[146] Accordingly, he cautioned Rakhal against visiting Vrindavana, the sacred place of Kṛṣṇa's boyhood exploits, lest the shock of re-cognition permanently establish him in his true nature and prevent him from returning to the mundane world.[147]

We have already seen the visiting *tāntrika* interpreting the "stem" and "flowers" of *kuṇḍalinī* yoga as Śiva's phallus and the Goddess's vagina. Ramakrishna could have arrived at a very similar interpretation as a result of his own "secret" awakening of the "coiled one" (*kuṇḍalinī*) in which he saw himself licking lotuses "shaped like vaginas" (*yonirūpa*):[148]

> This is very secret talk (*atiguhya kathā*)! I saw a boy of twenty-two or twenty-three exactly like me, going up the subtle channel, erotically playing with the vagina-shaped lotuses with his tongue! First the Anus, then the Phallus, then the Navel, the Four-petalled, the Six-petalled, the Ten-petalled—they were all drooping—now they became aroused! ... Ever since then I have been in this state.

From the fact that he appeared as a boy "of twenty-two or twenty-three," we can conclude that the symbolism of this vision stems back to the time Ramakrishna spent with the Bhairavī and his tutelage in "the sixty-four Tantras" under her.[149] Why the Ramakrishna-*homunculus* is using his tongue and not his penis is a matter of speculation. The fact that Ramakrishna was horrified at the thought of actual intercourse, indeed, that he seemed incapable of it (his "organ" was said to pull back up into its sheath, like the limbs of a tortoise, if he was touched by a "lewd woman"[150]), goes a long way in explaining Ramakrishna's preference for visionary cunnilingus over intercourse. But not far enough. After all, Ramakrishna once compared men attached to "woman-and-gold" to the jackals and dogs who "wet their faces" in their mates' behinds,[151] not a particularly positive assessment of oral contact with the vagina. And *where* would have he gotten the image of himself licking vagina-shaped lotuses? His stray comments that the Bhairavī "forced" him into strange and repulsive rituals is revealing.[152] One could speculate that some form of ritualized cunnilingus is all the Bhairavī could manage to get out of Ramakrishna, who invariably went into ecstasy every time he was placed in his ritual partner's lap, effectively making ritual intercourse redundant.[153] One could also speculate that Ramakrishna's tongue has something to do with the "cosmic vagina" (*brahmayoni*), "lolling" (*lak lak karā*) like Kālī's tongue, that he saw under the banyan tree during his Tantric *sādhana*. Another lolling tongue, this time of fire, once came out of Ramakrishna in a vision and tasted all things—feces, urine, cooked food—with its fiery licks, proving for Ramakrishna that "everything is one, undivided."[154] The tongue, then, associated in his visions with oral sex, with tongue-like lolling vaginas, and with the basic unity and purity of all things, is an eminently Tantric organ, establishing by what it does (ritual sex is an integral part of Tantric practice), by its shape (the vagina is worshipped in Tantric ritual), and by what it tastes (otherwise unlawful substances are consumed in Tantric ritual), that "everything is one, undivided," even something as impure and defiled as that "hated place" (*ghṛnār sthāna*),[155] the vagina. And so, by licking lotuses shaped like vaginas, Ramakrishna establishes a basic Tantric dictum: *everything* is pure.[156] Whatever the origin of the vision's material, one thing is clear: the experience that Ramakrishna identified as the beginning of his more or less permanent mystical state was an experience symbolically loaded with erotic connotations: the Ramakrishna-*homunculus* wasn't "communing" with innocent lotuses, as Nikhilananda would have us believe,[157] but engaging in a mystical form of oral sex, arousing vagina-shaped lotuses into ecstatic blossoms with a playful Tantric tongue.

Ramakrishna took these same lotuses and identified particular disciples with them in a manner similar to that in which presiding deities are placed on them in the yoga manuals and Tantras. Narendra, for example, was compared to the *sahasrāra-cakra*, the Thousand-petalled lotus in the head where Śiva sits waiting for his lover, the Goddess Śakti.[158] Ramakrishna's comments, then, that, whenever he looked at Narendra his mind "dissolved in the Undivided," is instructive, as this is exactly what is supposed to happen when the Goddess Śakti finally reaches the Thousand-petalled lotus and unites with her lover, Śiva. Ramakrishna was, in effect, identifying Narendra with Śiva himself in the Thousand-petalled lotus *of Ramakrishna's own subtle body.* Narendra was thus, indeed, a "part" of Ramakrishna, with whom Ramakrishna, as the feminine Śakti, united in the subtle body of the communal incarnation.

Not everyone, however, was impressed with Ramakrishna's erotic community, dancing naked before one another, paired up into couples, identified with Caitanya's disciples, and located on lotuses for Ramakrishna to unite with. Narendra's relatives don't like the fact that Narendra is seeing Ramakrishna. Narendra's aunt scolds the older Surendra for paying Narendra's carriage fee to Dakshineshwar.[159] Surendra warns Ramakrishna that Rakhal's father could sue him, for Rakhal is a minor.[160] Another man accuses Ramakrishna of inordinately "loving the boys."[161] Narayan is beat up by his family when he returns home from visiting Ramakrishna; Ramakrishna jokingly suggests that he buy a leather-jacket to absorb the blows.[162] In another passage, a piqued Ramakrishna scolds little Naren for abandoning his studies to visit him: "Your father will hurt you."[163] Paltu is also in trouble for seeing Ramakrishna.[164] Ramakrishna asks M if he could go to M's school to look for boys. M suggests that, instead Ramakrishna wait at his house and that he bring the boys to him.[165] But the parents catch on to M's tricks, and M is in trouble.[166] This sort of maneuvering won M the title of "the kidnapping teacher," a title jokingly bestowed by the boys and accepted by Ramakrishna as appropriate.[167] In another passage, Ramakrishna notes that Captain, an older disciple, is slandering the boys for visiting him. "Perhaps Hazra has slandered them before the Captain," Ramakrishna speculates.[168] And finally, Girish Ghosh once confessed that seeing Ramakrishna "playing" with a young boy reminded him of a "terrible canard" that he had once heard about the saint.[169]

As Obeyesekere has pointed out, there is no "native viewpoint" on a subject, only conflicting views that spar and fight in the "debate" that characterizes any culture and its act of self-interpretation.[170] What Isherwood called "the phenomenon"[171] of

Ramakrishna was certainly no exception—some worshipped him as a veritable incarnation of God; others kicked him with their boots for faking his ecstasies or beat their children who dared to visit him, leather-jacket or no.[172] Having looked at this "debate" as it has been recorded in the *Kathāmṛta*, let us turn now to the present and our own academic concerns, and try to locate ourselves somewhere within its discourse.

6. *An Interpretation of Ramakrishna's Foot*

We began with Ramakrishna's foot provocatively placed in a boy's lap. We tentatively took it as an embodied symbol of the mystico-erotic base of Ramakrishna's religious experiences, what we have called "the secret of Ramakrishna," and then proceeded to see whether the rest of the text supported our initial reading. It did. But what have we really accomplished? What does it mean to say that Ramakrishna's mystical experiences were "erotic," that in the very midst of an ecstatic state, supposedly "without a tinge of lust,"[173] Ramakrishna's foot, quite independently of Ramakrishna, found its way into the genitals of another human being? Surely we must ask, with M, why Ramakrishna's hair stands on end when he thinks about "little Naran,"[174] or smile when Ramakrishna brags that "I have never slept with a woman, even in a dream"[175]—so infatuated with boys, we might ask, what need did he have of women? But putting aside such doubts and smiles, we are still left with a very serious question: what does it mean to say that Ramakrishna's mystical experiences were "erotic"?

To get at this question we will adopt the dialectical hermeneutics of Gananath Obeyesekere, who in his book, *The Work of Culture*, picks up the path Ricoeur traced in his *Freud and Philosophy*[176] and attempts a synthesis of Freud's psychoanalytic program and more recent work in anthropology and the history of religions. Obeyesekere sums up Ricoeur's thesis well:[177]

> Freudianism, Ricoeur argues, essentially deals with the archaic substrate of a symbolic form in a regressive movement. Yet implicit in Freud's theory of sublimation is

> the *progressive* transformation of infantile and archaic motivations into art, religion, and public culture. Progression and regression are dialectical movements that may be found in such elemental expressions as dreams and fantasy, and in more complex ways in numinous religious symbols. ... *A progressive movement of unconscious thoughts involves the transformation of the archaic motivations of childhood into symbols that look forward to the resolution of conflict and beyond that into the nature of the sacred or numinous.* This double movement of symbols permits the theoretical reconciliation of the Freudian hermeneutics as illusion which has to be deciphered in terms of archaic motivations, with the phenomenology of religion of Leenhardt, Eliade, and others, for whom the symbol must be deciphered as a "revelation of the sacred."

Building on this program, Obeyesekere writes of what he calls "personal symbols," which he defines as "cultural symbols that are related to individual motivation and make sense only in relation to the life history of the individual."[178] As a personal symbol carries public, communicable meanings, it makes sense to the culture at large, but it remains undeciphered until we relate it to the individual life-history in which it occurs and reveal its uniquely personal dimensions, its secrets. Sometimes we find only "symptoms," one-way signs that suggest a neurosis fixated on an unresolved crisis. But sometimes, in exceptional cases, we find genuine two-way "symbols" that function *both* as symptoms, harking back to the original crisis, *and* as numinous symbols, pointing to greater meaning and what Obeyesekere calls "a radical transformation of one's being."[179] Obeyesekere identifies Ramakrishna as one of those "exceptional cases" in which the symptom became a symbol and turned a crisis into an experience of the sacred:[180]

> Consider the case of the great Hindu mystic, Ramakrishna, who ... was possessed by Kali and constantly saw her in visions. Ramakrishna's Hinduism permits the progressive development of the personal symbol ... To Ramakrishna his own mother is mother Kali who is *the* Mother and the

> guiding principle of cosmic creativity. Through Kali, Ramakrishna has achieved trance and knowledge of a radically different order from the others, and he can progress to the heart of a specifically Hindu reality that is essentially salvific.

What Ramakrishna achieved "through Kali" we will deal with in more detail elsewhere.[181] Here what he achieved "through Kṛṣṇa" is much more relevant, for it was a specifically Vaiṣṇava mythology that legitimated and supported Ramakrishna's homoerotic relationships with his disciples. But "becoming Rādhā" did much more than simply legitimate an otherwise suspect homosexual tendency—it *transformed* the attraction itself, gave it a specifically sacred dimension, and so allowed it to burst forth into rapture, vision, and song: "A progressive movement of unconscious thoughts involves the transformation of the archaic motivations of childhood into symbols that look forward to the resolution of conflict and beyond that into the nature of the sacred or numinous."[182] In effect, Ramakrishna took the anxious energies (*vyākulatā*) of his early sexual crisis, a crisis for which he almost killed himself, and "turned them around the corner"[183] until the purple and crimson dawn of anxious desire broke into the brilliant light of mystical experience. In Obeyesekere's terms, he took what were regressive symptoms and converted them into progressive symbols, into genuine experiences of a sacred, mystical realm. The change was a radical one: having once attempted to castrate himself symbolically with Kālī's sword for feeling "a strange sensation in the breast," he now compares his love for his male disciples to a mystical phallus. With a stray glance or a mere brush of bodies, Ramakrishna now finds himself "dissolved in the Undivided," uniting with his beloved Narendra in the Thousand-petalled lotus floating in Ramakrishna's own subtle body, interestingly enough, in the head. Ramakrishna is now an *ūrdhvaretā,* one whose erotic energies have "turned up" away from the genitals and into the head.[184] He has become, as he claimed, a mystical phallus aroused into ecstasy "by the slightest things."[185] The lopped off, castrated head swinging in Kālī's hand has become Śiva's phallus, bold and sure in its erection, "thrust straight up from the underworld," till, as a phallic stem, it unites with its lotus in the very same head Ramakrishna once threatened to cut off. "Sublimation" is too weak a word for what has happened. "Libidinal energies" have not been "sublimated" in a transformation that never quite escapes its materialistic origins; rather, a mystico-erotic energy called *śakti* has been "awakened," revealing to Ramakrishna that "She herself has become everything." The world is now experienced for *what it has been all along*, the body of the Goddess, physically, literally divine.

Here, then, is where we would locate the meaning of Ramakrishna's foot—*both* in his obvious infatuation for his boy disciples, an infatuation somehow connected with the archaic "regressive" motivations of his own personal history, *and* in a "progressive," essentially mystical, order of rapture and vision, the realm of the sacred and the numinous. By a deft use of religious symbolism, Ramakrishna was able to use his homoerotic desires as the driving force of his mystical life: *what was once a crisis became the secret of his mystical and charismatic success.* His foot is an embodied symbol of this secret, of this dialectical movement back and forth between the regressive and the progressive, a movement that turned a young lonely man despairing of his life into a charismatic religious leader surrounded by some of Calcutta's most talented men, young and old.

And again, it is this same dialectical nature that we have in mind when we describe Ramakrishna's religious experiences as "erotic." We use the term in a very specific way. Because of its long history in Platonic and Christian mystical discourse, "the erotic" is capable of carrying mystical connotations, similar to those Ramakrishna would understand and enthusiastically accept. But because of its common usage in contemporary American culture, it can also imply sexual fantasy and arousal, the stuff of psychoanalysis. In other words, it can be used *both* in an essentially mystical "progressive" sense *and* in a psychoanalytically defined "regressive" sense. "The erotic" is thus a third, specifically methodological, specifically dialectical, category where the horizons of religious experience and psychoanlysis can meet in the act of interpretation. As a dialectical term refusing to separate the sexual and the mystical, it also mirrors the Indian category of *śakti*, a term which can mean everything from "magical power," to "talent," to "physical force," to the mystical energy lying dormant at the base of the spine waiting to uncoil and wind its way up through the different centers—the Anus, the Phallus, the Navel—until it can unite with its lover in the head. This whole, essentially Tantric, symbolism demands a wholistic understanding of human energies, capable of incorporating everything from sexual desire to formless mystical experience under one interpretive category. "The erotic" is the closest we can come in the English language, for it harbors hints of Freud's omnipresent *libido,* infinite in its magical transformations, as well as Pseudo-Dionysius' *Divine Eros,* enticed away from its transcendent dwelling place to dwell within all things and yet, by virtue of its supernatural and ecstatic capacity, remaining within itself, turning "from itself and through itself and upon itself and toward itself in an everlasting circle."[186] And finally, the term's Platonic origins and connotations—*eros* as a homoerotic love of boys sublimated into a vision of the divine—is particularly appropriate when we come to Ramakrishna's unique use of his homoeroticism as a mystical technique. Ramakrishna's love for his boys was truly "Platonic," not in the sense in which it is used today—a love devoid of passion—but in the sense Plato used it in his *Phaedrus* and *Symposium*—a homoerotic infatuation harnessed and "winged" for ecstatic flight. Ramakrishna's love was a love at once sexual and mystical, an "erotic" love.

Admittedly, one could read Ramakrishna's foot and the whole erotic mysticism it symbolizes as "nothing but" repressed sexuality, understood in its most positivistic sense. But such a move simply makes no sense in the Tantric world within which, we are convinced, Ramakrishna's secret must be interpreted. In the monistic world of Tantra, where a conscious energy called *śakti* constitutes everything that is, where "She has become everything," debasing one form of energy, the mystical, by "reducing" it to another, the sexual, is a hopeless and meaningless enterprise. As Ramakrishna saw in a vision, *everything* is vibrating as this conscious energy, from the walls to a stray cat.[187] To the charge, then, that his mystical experiences are transformed sexual energies, the *tāntrika* would simply reply: "Of course. And sexual energies are *deformed* mystical energies." Psychoanalysis *is* helpful because it allows us to identify certain dynamics and to ask interesting questions, but we are mistaken if we think that simply because we use psychoanalytic insights we must, therefore, adopt the early twentieth century materialism that Freud happened to espouse. Not so. Indian Tantra makes very similar claims and recognizes very similar processes, but it operates in a completely different metaphysical order, one that is quite capable of incorporating much of psychoanalysis without surrendering its own mystical worldview. As one *tāntrika* put it, Freud only got to the third *cakra*.

The hermeneutical task is complicated by the fact that Ramakrishna resolutely rejected Tantra as "the latrine of the house"[188] through which one can, indeed, enter the house of mystical experience, but only after being greatly defiled. Despite this profound ambivalence toward Tantra, however, Ramakrishna consistently saw Tantric images and performed Tantric acts in his ecstatic states. Indeed, if we are to judge by the number of times his ecstasies were associated with actual defecation, erotic imagery, or symbolically erotic acts, we might conclude that "the latrine of the house" was *precisely* the "door" through which Ramakrishna entered. His foot, a symbolically erotic act *within* a mystical state, is yet another example of his unacknowledged Tantra. The fact that he denied having anything to do with this foot suggests that Ramakrishna's foot was an unconscious foot and Ramakrishna himself an unconscious *tāntrika*, profoundly uncomfortable in a Tantric world. As he questioned the basic dictum of Tantra—that sex and mystical experience are intimately related, even identical on some deep energetic level—Ramakrishna lacked the hermeneutical key with which to interpret his oddly placed foot, his disconcerting attraction for boys, and the contents of his strange "secret" visions. Unable to interpret them for himself, Ramakrishna asked others to explain his visions and "strange sensations" for him. His disciples did their best, and we have done our's, not by reducing Ramakrishna's secret to some mechanical *libido*, but by trying to relate it to Tantra and its dialectical understanding of the mystical and the erotic. We have used psychoanalytic categories, but only as tools that can supplement and enrich those of Tantra, already perfectly capable of seeing a penis and a vagina in the stem and flower of a lotus.

But still, perhaps we have left ourselves too open to the charge of only having "rubbed our touchstone against the lotus"[189]—perhaps we have attempted to understand what were exquisite and delicate experiences, feminine flowers, with clumsy categories and unfeeling tools, our hard masculine reasons. No doubt, Ramakrishna, who uttered half the *Kathāmṛta* "with a smile," would laugh at us and our touchstones. But we try anyway, knowing that when all is said and done, Ramakrishna's secret must remain a secret, his to experience, ours to ponder and to interpret from afar.

---

[1] We are using the thirty-first edition of the Kathāmṛta Bhavana five-volume set: Mahendranath Gupta, *Śrīśrīrāmakṛṣṇakathāmṛta* (Calcutta: Kathāmṛta Bhavana, 1987). We will reference it as KA and will give both the date of the conversation, so that the reader can go to the English translation if desired, and the volume and page number of the Bengali text. All translations are my own.

[2] Swami Nikhilananda (trans.), *The Gospel of Sri Ramakrishna* (New York: Ramakrishna-Vivekananda Center, 1984).

[3] Swami Saradananda, *Śrīśrīrāmakṛṣṇalīlāprasaṅga* (Calcutta: Udbodhana Karyalaya, 1986). We will reference it as LP, followed by the part, section, and paragraph numbers.

[4] Swami Jagadananda (trans.), *Sri Ramakrishna: The Great Master* (Mylapore: Sri Ramakrishna Math, 1978).

[5] See my "Revealing and Concealing the Secret: A Textual History of Mahendranath Gupta's *Śrīśrīrāmakṛṣṇakathāmṛta*" in *South Asia: Occasional Papers*, no. 40 (East Lansing: Asian Studies Center, Michigan State University, 1991).

[6] I am indebted to Narasingha Sil for this bit of word-play.

[7] What Gupta held back is impossible to say, as the diaries from which he edited the *Kathāmṛta* are off-limits to scholars. Gupta's family possesses the actual manuscripts while the Ramakrishna Order possesses a complete set of photographs. Neither body is willing to open the diaries to public inquiry. Secrets still are being concealed.

[8] Nikhilananda, *The Gospel*, p. vii.

[9] I am presently researching and writing a dissertation entitled "Kālī's Child: The Mystical and the Erotic in Mahendranath Gupta's *Śrīśrīrāmakṛṣṇakathāmṛta*," of which this article will be a part.

[10] April 22, 1886; KA 2.231.

[11] See Wendy O'Flaherty, *The Rig Veda* (New York: Penguin, 1981), pp. 30-31.

[12] April 15, 1983; KA 2.38.

[13] October 27, 1885; KA 1.254. A doctor takes Ramakrishna's feet as a sign of defeat on October 26, 1885; KA 1.238.

[14] Appendix; KA 1.258.

[15] October 25, 1885; KA 1.232.

[16] December 14, 1982; KA 1.73. It is, however, acceptable to take a job in order to support one's mother (June 15, 1884; KA 1.122).

[17] LP 2.14.9.

[18] March 11, 1885; KA 1.197, *et. al.*

[19] April 18, 1886; KA 4.292. See also October 27, 1885 in KA 1.246, and March 11, 1883 in KA 2.22.

[20] October 16, 1882; KA 2.4.

[21] June 5, 1883; KA 2.59.

[22] August 27, 1885; KA 4.245.

[23] June 8, 1883; KA 4.21.

[24] June 4, 1883; KA 2.53-54.

[25] The tradition is split on whether it was Ramakrishna's right foot or his hand that sent the young Narendra into ecstasy. Narendra is recorded in the traditional biographies—Saradananda's *Śrīśrīrāmakṛṣṇalīlāprasaṅga* (1911-18), the Order's *Life of Sri Ramakrishna* (1924), and Rolland's *The Life of Sri Ramakrishna* (1929)—as saying that it was Ramakrishna's right foot, but the *Kathāmṛta* records Ramakrishna as saying that he used his hand (March 7, 1885 in KA 3.117; May 9, 1885 in KA 3.161).

[26] Ramakrishna places his foot on Narendra's knee again on September 29, 1885 in KA 2.138.

[27] February 22, 1885; KA 5.128-131.

[28] July 13, 1885; KA 4.215.

[29] October 25, 1885; KA 1.226.

[30] October 27, 1885; KA 1.254. See also October 26, 1885; KA 1.240, where Ramakrishna suggests that Sarkar's doubts are the result of his having read too much "science-fience nonsense."

[31] In M's English translation of 1907, M has Sarkar saying, "Well, Sir, may I say that it is not good that you allow people during *Samadhi* to touch Your feet with their body?" (M, *Gospel of Sri Ramakrishna* [Madras: Brahmavadin Office, 1907], p. 362). Apparently, the act bothered M as well, at least enough for him to want to attribute its agency to someone other than Ramakrishna when he presented it to an English-speaking public.

[32] At one point, M adopts Girish's position, calling Ramakrishna's sufferings a "crucifixion" in which Ramakrishna "sacrifices his body for the devotees" (March 14, 1886; KA 3.249).

[33] October 31, 1885; KA 2.218.

[34] October 31, 1885; KA 4.275.

[35] October 31, 1885; KA 4.278. It should be pointed out that it is not until volume three that the lap (*kola*) is specified as an object of Ramakrishna's foot (May 23, 1885; KA 3.172). In earlier volumes, Ramakrishna touches "bodies" (*ga*) or "chests" (*buka*). This is a subtle example of the layering effect structuring the five volumes and its attempt to conceal a secret that I wrote about in my "Revealing and Concealing the Secret."

[36] José Cabezón and Sudhir Kakar have pointed out to me that this is a Hindu model as well—great gurus can vicariously absorb another person's sins. Without denying the possible Hindu roots of Girish's theology, I would nevertheless insist on the predominantly Christian roots of this idea as it was presented by M in the *Kathāmṛta*. What needs to be shown is the manner in which Ramakrishna was interpreted and presented *with a Western or Western-educated audience in mind.* The patterning of Ramakrishna as another Jesus, who takes upon himself the sins of others, is one aspect of this apologetic project. When M, for example, comments that some considered Ramakrishna's final sufferings to be a "Crucifixion" in which Ramakrishna "sacrificed his body for the sake of the devotees" (March 14, 1886; KA 3.249), it is very clear that M does not have Indian gurus in mind as his theological models.

[37] LP 2.6.1.

[38] "Decapitate" may seem too strong a word here, but we must remember that Ramakrishna was about to use Kālī's sacrificial sword, which was used to ritually decapitate sacrificial goats. It should also be noted that, alongside human sacrifice, which was also practiced, self-decapitation holds a legitimate place in the Kālī cult, where it was sometimes used by devotees to show their profound devotion for the Goddess. Kālī, after all, wears a garland of lopped off heads around her neck and holds a decapitated head and a sacrificial sword in her two left hands.

[39] LP 2.6.13.

[40] The expression is M's (October 26, 1884; KA 1.175).

[41] July 3, 1884; KA 4.113, *et. al.*

[42] June 4, 1883, KA 2.48; November 28, 1883, KA 2.73-74, *et al.*

[43] March 7, 1884; KA 3.126.

[44] March 11, 1885; KA 1.188. Nikhilananda omits this scene.

[45] March 11, 1885; KA 1.192.

[46] April 6, 1885; KA 3.131.

[47] I am indebted to Narasingha Sil for this linguistic note (personal conversation).

[48] June 13, 1885; KA 3.182.

[49] October 30, 1885; KA 3.224.

[50] April 12, 1885; KA 3.149.

[51] October 27, 1885; KA 4.271. It should be pointed out here that this day was "split" by M in order to conceal this "secret" confession. The afternoon conversation of the day was recorded in the very first volume (1902), whereas the morning session, when the confession occurred, was kept for the fourth (1910). Again, along with "the body" in the earlier volumes becoming "the lap" in volume three, this is a good example of the layering effect that I have analyzed in my "Revealing and Concealing the Secret."

[52] Nikhilananda, *The Gospel*, p. 895.

[53] LP 2.6.13.

[54] LP 4.4.47.

[55] LP 4.5.5.

[56] LP 5.5.13. See also 5.5.14.

[57] LP 5.3.6.

[58] Carl Olson makes a very similar interpretation of Kālī's sword and garland of heads in a different context, Ramakrishna's retracting penis, in his *The Mysterious Play of Kālī: An Interpretive Study of Rāmakrishna* (Atlanta: Scholars Press, 1990), p. 34.

[59] Gananath Obeyesekere, *The Work of Culture: Symbolic Transformation in Psychoanalysis and Anthropology* (Chicago: University of Chicago Press, 1990), p. 24. See below for a more extended treatment of Obeyesekere's "personal symbol" as applied to Ramakrishna.

[60] July 15, 1885; KA 4.232.

[61] We base our guess on another passage, this time in volume five, where Ramakrishna reveals more of his "secret talk": "I'm telling you something very secret (*atiguhya kathā*). In order to conquer lust I performed many rituals. For example, shouting 'Victory to Kālī! 'Victory to Kālī!', I walked around the seat of bliss many times" (December 14, 1882; KA 5.25). Because "the seat of bliss" has something to do with "lust" (*kāma*), we conclude that it refers to the Bhairavī's lap. Again, it is curious that a confession that occurred so early in M's relationship with Ramakrishna was not recorded for the public until volume five, published in 1932, the year M died. It was omitted completely by Nikhilananda (Nikhilananda, *The Gospel*, 161).

[62] July 15, 1885; 4.231. Nikhilananda mistranslates this: "I used to joke with him" (Nikhilananda, *The Gospel*, 813).

[63] July 15, 1885; KA 4.232. Nikhilananda completely omits this confession (Nikhilananda, *The Gospel*, 814).

[64] July 15, 1885; KA 4.227-28. See also March 9, 1884; KA 5.114.

[65] October 10, 1883; KA 5.83. See also June 13, 1885; KA 3.183.

[66] May 24, 1884; KA 5.122.

[67] June 13, 1885; KA 3.179.

[68] Both phrases occur in M's section heading, *ibid.*

[69] April 24, 1885; KA 2.207.

[70] October 23, 1885; KA 4.259.

[71] June 4, 1883; KA 2.47.

[72] March 9, 1883; KA 5.30-31.

[73] October 11, 1884; KA 2.154; See also March 11, 1883; KA 2.14.

[74] June 4, 1883; KA 2.49-50.

[75] September 26, 1884; KA 2.125.

[76] April 16, 1886; KA 2.228. Nikhilananda covers up Ramakrishna's flirtatious Rādhā by describing her as "a romantic" (Nikhilananda, *The Gospel*, p. 957).

[77] Jagadananda (trans.), *The Great Master*, p. 183, fn 1.

[78] "Do you know why Kṛṣṇa is thrice-bent? For love of Rādhā." (December 6, 1884; KA 5.196).

[79] June 4, 1883; KA 2.49.

[80] February 2, 1884; KA 4.63, and March 9, 1884; KA 5.107. The number of visions and ecstasies that occurred "on the way to the pine grove" or in the pine grove itself is striking and calls for serious comment.

[81] February 24, 1884; KA 4.75. See also March 23, 1884; KA 4.80.

[82] The phrase *bhāvei thāk* is a complicated one, as it could and *does* mean both "Remain in the world" and "Remain in ecstasy." What it means, then, is "Remain between the world and the divine, poised in the realization that the two are one." As such, it is an essentially Tantric state, dialectically uniting the opposites in what Ramakrishna called *bhāvamukha*, "having one's face turned toward *bhāva* ("the world" *or* "ecstasy")," a sort of "mystical two-facedness."

[83] January 1, 1883; KA 4.3.

[84] November 28, 1883; KA 2.74 *et. al.*

[85] There is a real problem in determining the gender of the divine in Ramakrishna's language since *Bengali pronouns do not distinguish gender.* The result is a very fluid religious world in which a masculine "Lord" (*iśvara*), a feminine Goddess, and a neuter Absolute (*brahman*) all are referred to by the pronoun *tini*, "he," "she," *or* "it." Consequently, context is everything. We translate the pronoun here as "He" since the theological model being used is a theistic (Vaiṣṇava) one in which God commonly is referred to as masculine.

[86] September 21, 1884; KA 2.116.

[87] November 28, 1883; KA 1.115

[88] "I said to Kedar, 'Nothing will happen if your mind dwells on woman-and-gold.' I wanted to pass my hand over his breast, but I could not. It was all knotted up inside. I could not enter a room that smelled of shit" (July 15, 1885; KA 4.230).

[89] For a convincing study of Ramakrishna's atttitude towards "the job" (*cakari*), see Sumit Sarkar's analysis of the social dimensions of Ramakrishna's language and symbolism in his "The Kathamrita as Text: Towards an Understanding of Ramakrishna Paramahamsa," *Occasional Papers on History and Society*, number XXII (New Delhi: Nehru Memorial Museum and Library, 1985), p. 63ff.

[90] February 2, 1884; KA 4.68.

[91] July 3, 1884; KA 4.109. Whose body is allowed to touch whose reveals a great deal about Ramakrishna. For example, whereas he had no problem with all the caressing, massaging, and bathing going on between himself and his boy disciples, Ramakrishna condemned the "rubbing of bodies" (*gāyer gharṣaṇa*) that occurs between a husband and wife in bed—it produces too much "heat" (July 13, 1885; KA 4.214).

[92] March 11, 1885; KA 1.188. Balaram's house is described as a "temple" in the Order's 1986 edition, *Śrīśrīrāmakṛṣṇakathāmṛta* (Calcutta: Udbodhana Karyalaya, 1986), p. 887.

[93] September 21, 1884; KA 2.121. M, guessing his reader's thoughts, is quick to explain what Ramakrishna meant: "If he would have looked at the boy any longer, the Master would have become lost in ecstasy." Nikhilananda, fearing his reader's thoughts, completely omits Ramakrishna's words and instead puts M's gloss in Ramakrishna's mouth: "I should have been overwhelmed with ecstasy if he had stayed here a little longer" (Nikhilananda, *The Gospel*, p. 556).

[94] March 11, 1883; KA 2.24. Nikhilananda tones the passage down and gives it a specifically religious dimension by translating *uddīpana* as "inspired," a lexically appropriate translation (Nikhilananda, *The Gospel*, p. 194). The word literally means "enkindled" or "lighting up" but often can best be translated as "reminded." For example, when Ramakrishna sees an English boy leaning up against a tree, he is "reminded of Kṛṣṇa" (*śrīkṛṣner uddīpana*) (June 4, 1883; KA 2.49). Similarly, when he sees a prostitute dressed in blue sitting under a tree, he becomes "completely enkindled" (*dapa kare ekebāre*) and is "reminded of Sītā" (*sītār uddīpana*) (ibid.). We would only insist that what "inspired" or "enkindled" Ramakrishna's religious ecstasies and visions also erotically "excited" him. Religious inspiration and erotic excitement cannot be separated in Ramakrishna,

nor can one somehow be reduced to the other. Ramakrishna's *uddīpana*, then, was at once religious "inspiration," mythical "rememberance," and erotic "excitement." It was the erotic that "lighted up" (*uddīpana*) the mythical imagination and sparked Ramakrishna's mystical states. Or in Ramakrishna's words: "Looking at pictures of holy men and becoming excited (*uddīpana*) . . . is like a man looking at a young woman and having his desire aroused (*uddīpana*)" (May 24, 1884; KA 5.120).

95 March 7, 1885; KA 3.118.

96 Deceber 23, 1885; KA 4.280. Nikhilananda omits this scene.

97 The phrase is M's, who in his English translation of 1907 portrays Ramakrishna, "the Son of God," as another Jesus with Narendra as his "beloved disciple." The Christianization of Ramakrishna here is considerable, down to the King James English M used to present his Lord to an English-speaking public.

98 September 19, 1884; KA 4.163.

99 April 9, 1887; KA 3.273.

100 September 29, 1884; KA 2.138-139. Nikhilananda omits the entire scene.

101 April 13, 1886; KA 3.264. It was passages like this one that Jeffrey M. Masson recorded (in end notes) as evidence for "the blatant homosexual concerns of Ramakrishna" ("The Oceanic Feeling: Origin of the Term" in J. Moussaieff Masson, *The Oceanic Feeling: The Origins of Religious Sentiment in Ancient India* [Dordrecht: D. Reidel Publishing Company, 1980], pp. 46-47). Masson was the earliest scholar, of whom we am aware, to take serious note of Ramakrishna's homosexual dimensions.

102April 22, 1886; KA 2.236.

103 April 9, 1887; KA 3.275. See also May 8, 1887; KA 2.256.

104 October 16, 1882; KA 2.5. Nikhilananda tones the passage down by mistranslating "me" (āmāe) as "us": "You have made us so happy today!" (Nikhilananda, *The Gospel*, p. 121).

105 August 19, 1883; KA 1.99.

106 September 19, 1884; KA 4.163-164.

107 March 25, 1887; KA 3.267.

108 March 11, 1885, KA 1.201.

109 August 19, 1883, KA 1.102.

110 March 11, 1885; KA 1.204.

111 March 11, 1885; KA 1.207.

112 Ibid.

113 April 9, 1887; KA 3.274.

114 See April 9, 1887, KA 3.274 for M's version of the event. See Swami Prabhananda, *Ānandarūpa Śrīrāmakṛṣṇa* (Calcutta: Śilālipi, 1981), pp. 219-25, for background and an interpretation of the drawing. Prabhananda's scholarship on Ramakrishna is quite good and should be looked at more closely, as he is the only person alive that has had the opportunity to study in detail the actual diary manuscripts from which M created the *Kathāmṛta* (see my "Revealing and Concealing the Secret").

[115] September 21, 1884; KA 2.110 and November 9, 1884; KA 3.94. See also September 21, 1884 in KA 2.117 for Kṛṣṇa's arched peacock feather cap arousing Rādhā's heart.

[116] August 9, 1885; KA 4.239. Ramakrishna, however, complains to Kālī about Keshab's "English opinions." "Such will it be in the *Kali yuga* (the last and most corrupt of the world ages)," the Goddess explains to him.

[117] October 4, 1884; KA 4.193.

[118] August 18, 1883; KA 5.62. Nikhilananda omits M's question (Nikhilananda, *The Gospel*, 273).

[119] Both expressions may be based on a well-known myth in which Brahmā and Viṣṇu are arguing over who is the greater god when a huge *Śiva-liṅgam* materializes, burning in space. In order to measure its immensity, Brahmā flies up and Viṣṇu plunges down, but neither can fathom its end—Śiva's *liṅgam* is endless, "thrust straight up from the underworld" and "stretching even down to Benares." The two gods are roundly defeated.

[120] October 1, 1884; KA 2.147. See also August 18, 1883; KA 5.62.

[121] Narasingha Sil is under the opinion that "the pearl" refers to a small ball of semen carefully teased out of the erect penis in an act of ritual masturbation (Narasingha P. Sil, *Ramakṛṣṇa Paramahaṁsa: A Psychological Profile* [Leiden: E.J. Brill, 1991], p. 51). Nikhilananda omits this "pearl" from his translation. As with most of Nikhilananda's omissions, this one is just as revealing as it is concealing: if "the pearl" does not refer to a ball of semen, then why did Nikhilananda choose to omit it?

[122] July 3, 1884; KA 4.106.

[123] In *kuṇḍalinī* yoga, an attempt is made to awaken "the serpent power" lying "coiled up" (*kuṇḍalinī*) at the base of the *suṣumna*, a subtle channel running from the anus to the top of the skull. Once awakened, the feminine energy (*śakti*) shoots up the channel, piercing lotus-like *cakras* ("wheels" or "lotuses") as she goes until she finally reaches the "thousand-petalled" (*sahasrāra*) lotus in the head and unites there with her lover, Śiva.

[124] January 2, 1884; KA 5.103.

[125] September 29, 1884; KA 2.136. Ramakrishna was wearing nothing "around his waist," M tells us.

[126] October 17, 1882; KA 2.7.

[127] July 15, 1885; KA 4.227.

[128] November 9, 1884; KA 3.99. This might help explain why Ramakrishna often objected to women taking part in the singing and dancing (cf. November 9, 1884; KA 3.98).

[129] October 26, 1885; KA 1.237.

[130] October 16, 1882; KA 2.2. See also LP 2.6.6.

[131] September 26, 1883; KA 2.67.

[132] March 7, 1885; KA 3.119.

[133] March 7, 1885; KA 3.124.

[134] July 13, 1885; KA 4.212.

[135] June 20, 1884; KA 4.98.

136 June 20, 1884; KA 4.99.

137 July 13, 1885; KA 4.214. Rakhal and Niranjana also have masculine natures (June 20, 1884; KA 4.100).

138 July 15, 1885; KA 4.228.

139 Ibid.

140 September 19, 1884; KA 4.164. See also June 5, 1883 in KA 2.58, where it is explained why Bhavanath is the "woman" and Narendra the "man": "Bhavanath obediently follows Narendra."

141 December 23, 1885; KA 4.283. The "providers" provide material and economic support. Ramakrishna, who moved quite comfortably in the upper echelons of nineteenth-century Calcutta society, never lacked his. From a sociological perspective, it is interesting to note that Ramakrishna took the synchronous presence and support of these "providers" as proof of the genuineness of his visions and ecstasies (June 4, 1883; KA 2.49).

142 July 13, 1885; KA 213.

143 M's speculation was shared by Ramakrishna, who liked to theologize with word-plays: *pūrṇa* means "full" or "complete."

144 This vision is recounted numerous times: December 9, 1883 (KA 2.82); December 24, 1883 (KA 4.45); August 9, 1884 (KA 4.239); December 23, 1885 (KA 4.283).

145 Advaita and Nityananda were Caitanya's two major disciples. It should also be pointed out that "Advaita," "Caitanya," and "Nityananda" could also be interpreted as states of consciousness: "the nondual," "awakened consciousness," and "the bliss of the eternal." As Saradananda points out, Ramakrishna's words often have more than one meaning (LP 4.3.11).

146 LP 5.2.14. This is another example of how Ramakrishna's visions and thoughts, much like dreams in a psychoanalytic framework, were formed by a linguistic playfulness: *rākhāla* means "cowherd boy."

147 Ibid.

148 August 9, 1885; KA 4.238. Another version occurrs on December 23, 1885 in KA 4.283.

149 Ramakrishna allegedly went through all the disciplines of "the sixty-four Tantras" with the Bhairavī (LP 2.11.7).

150 LP 4.AP.8.

151 December 3, 1881; KA 5.215. Nikhalananda tones this down considerably by translating "wet their faces in" (*mukha jubare thāke*) as "revel in" (Nikhilananda, *The Gospel*, p. 1013).

152 See July 15, 1885 (KA 4.232) for Ramakrishna being "forced" and August 24, 1882 (KA 3.24) for Ramakrishna's descriptions of the Tantric rituals he performed as "very strange" (*bhārī uṭkaṭa*) and "repulsive" (*cālāki noe*).

153 The Bhairavī sometimes used other women to train her young disciple (LP 2.111.8 and 2.11.10).

154 September 7, 1883; KA 3.46.

155 September 9, 1883; KA 3.51. The context is interesting: Ramakrishna is explaining how a *tāntrika* drinks three drops of wine from his

partner's vagina in order to gain certain powers. Nikhilananda omits this observation.

156 I am indebted to my graduate advisor and mentor, Wendy Doniger, for this insight.

157 Nikhilananda has Ramakrishna "communing" with the lotuses with his tongue, despite the fact that the Bengali verb *ramaṇa karā* clearly implies a sexual act. There is no mention of the shape of the lotuses. Saradananda also conceals the erotic nature of the event, removing both the explicit verb and the shape of the lotuses from his account (LP 2.11.20).

158 July 15, 1885; KA 4.228.

159 September 26, 1883; KA 2.65.

160 September 7, 1884; KA 4.143.

161 October 2, 1884; KA 4.190. The phrase "loving the boys" is *chokarāder bhālavāsā*.

162 October 11, 1884; KA 2.157-158.

163 June 28, 1885; KA 3.196.

164 April 6, 1885; KA 3.129.

165 November 9, 1884; KA 3.101.

166 March 11, 1885; KA 1.192.

167 LP 5.7.29.

168 June 13, 1885; KA 3.180.

169 Sarkar, "The Kathamrita as a Text," p. 103.

170 Obeyesekere, *The Work of Culture*, pp. 219-225.

171 Christopher Isherwood, *Ramakrishna and His Disciples* (New York: Simon and Schuster, 1965), p. 1.

172 The manner in which M's *Kathāmṛta* preserves these conflicting opinions is a powerful argument for its historical accuracy, something we cannot always say for Saradananda's *Līlāprasaṅga*.

173 Literally "without even the smell of lust" (*kāmagandha vivarjita*)—the phrase is used in the *Kathāmṛta* to describe a perfected love free from sexual desire. For example, Ramakrishna described the love of the Vaiṣṇava poet Caṇḍīdās and his Tantric ritual partner, the washerwoman Rajakinī, as "without even the smell of lust" (January 4, 1884; KA 5.105 *et. al.*).

174 April 13, 1886; KA 3.263. Nikhilananda was afraid to ask this question with M, and so omitted it from his translation.

175 August 9, 1885; KA 4.240.

176 Paul Ricoeur, *Freud and Philosophy: An Essay on Interpretation* (New Haven: Yale University Press, 1970).

177 Obeyesekere, *The Work of Culture*, p. xviii, 17; second italics mine.

178 Ibid., p. 24.

179 Ibid.

180 Ibid., p. 21.

[181] As we pointed out earlier, the present essay is part of a larger project, one concerned largely with interpreting Ramakrishna through the iconography and mythology of Kālī.

[182] Obeyesekere, *The Work of Culture*, p. 17.

[183] The expression is one Ramakrishna often used to explain what one should do with the "inert" and "dark" (tāmasika) drives of human nature.

[184] For Ramakrishna's teaching on the *ūrdhvaretā* and how "one must hold the semen to attain God," see March 23, 1884 in KA 4.85.

[185] July 4, 1883; KA 2.49. The context is interesting: "the slightest thing" Ramakrishna is referring to is his worship of a fourteen year-old girl (*śundarī-pūjā*).

[186] Colm Luibheid and Paul Rorem (trans.), *Pseudo-Dionysius: The Complete Works* (New York: Paulist Press, 1987), pp. 82 and 84.

[187] December 16, 1883; KA 4.35.

[188] March 23, 1884; KA 5.181. The phrase "through the latrine of the house" (*pāikhānār madhya diyā*) is translated incorrectly by Nikhilananda as "through the back door" (Nikhilananda, *The Gospel*, 513). See also September 7, 1884; KA 4.134.

[189] The phrase is a taunt used by a sect of Bengali mystics, the Bauls, against proud scholars: "Who is this man, a dealer and expert in gold, that has entered the flower-garden? He rubs his touchstone against the lotus. Oh, the fun! Oh, the fun!" (quoted in Shashibhushan Dasgupta, *Obscure Religious Cults* [Calcutta: Firma KLM, 1976], p. 159).

V. Paul Gordon Schalow

Spiritual Dimensions of Male Beauty in Japanese Buddhism

1. Male Love as the Experience of Buddhist Mutability

During the 17th century in Japan, male writers of the samurai class produced a number of texts on the topic of male homosexual love. Male love as practiced by the samurai involved an adult man's love of a samurai youth. The sexual and emotional relationship conformed to a social construct called *shudô*, "the way of the youth," and 17th-century texts treating *shudô* defined both prescriptively and descriptively the nature of the man-youth relationship. These texts belonged to a genre of colloquial literature called *kana-zôshi,* books written in vernacular Japanese and employing a minimum of classical Chinese characters or locutions. One important characteristic of the genre, no matter what the topic, was that the books were meant to exhort and educate readers in moral behavior and, especially, the Confucian virtues.

The text translated here is unusual because it is Buddhist-inspired. The title is *The Record of Heartfelt Friends (Shin'yûki,* 1643).[1] The "heartfelt friend" (*shin'yû*) was the youthful lover in a man-youth relationship, *shin'yû* standing in juxtaposition to *nen'yû* (or *nenja*), the adult partner. The title thus suggests that the lessons contained in the book were primarily intended for the edification of samurai youths. The term "heartfelt friend" was apparently not a familiar one to most people of the day, for when a second edition of the book appeared in 1661, it was retitled *Tales of the Way of the Youth (Shudô monogatari*), employing the more familiar term *shudô*.[2] In any case, the appearance of a second edition speaks for the book's contemporary importance as a guide to the intricacies of "the way of the youth."

The Record of Heartfelt Friends takes the form of a Buddhist catechism in question/answer format, in which an enlightened master guides youths in the proper practice of "the way of the youth" by responding to their questions. The master's teachings can be summarized as follows: A man's lust for a youth is an expression of his appreciation of the mutability of adolescent male beauty. A youth's beauty attains metaphysical meaning when he responds to and relieves the lust his beauty generates in a man. The youth's ability to respond to a man is evidence of responsive love (*nasake*). Responsive love exists due to positive karmic virtue accrued from previous lives, and its exercise contributes in turn to "good" karma in the youth's future incarnations. Together, the man's lust and youth's relief of it serve as a form of Buddhist spiritual experience of mutability (*mujô*) and karmic destiny. To cynical modern ears this formula sounds self-serving and manipulative of youths, but to its original readership in the cultural and spiritual milieu of 17th-century Japan, the text represented a sincere explanation of the principles at work in the dynamic of love between man and youth.

2. *Description of The Catechism, Parts One and Two*

Part One of *The Record of Heartfelt Friends* begins with the master's soliloquy, describing his retirement from the vulgar world in search of the meaning of human existence. The master identifies the human heart as the source of all suffering and pain, and argues that our lives will only improve if "compassion (*jihi*) and love (*nasake*) are held in the highest regard by all people, from the ruler down to the common man." Buddhist compassion and love are directly equated, in typical syncretic fashion, to the five Confucian virtues: brotherhood, righteousness, ceremony, wisdom, and trust.

After thus establishing the preeminence of compassion and love, the master begins instruction on the nature of sexual love. He states that all human beings, male or female, priest or layman, are subject to sexual desire; this is a core truth of the human situation that simply cannot be escaped or denied. Given this fact, the master argues that satisfaction of desire is essential to human mental and emotional health. Those who suffer for the sake of love are described as superior to those who are unable to love, or who determine whom to love on the basis of the status of their would-be lover. To illustrate this last problem, the master introduces the cases of two remarkably handsome young men, one from China named Yü-hsin (dates unknown) and one from Japan named Noritoki (13th century), who lacked compassion and love in their dealings with the men who fell in love with them. In both cases, the cold-hearted youths were killed by the vengeful spirits of the men they spurned.

Here in the text, a question is interjected from a youth who asks why some youths such as Yü-hsin and Noritoki are, despite their physical beauty, incapable of responsive love. The master explains that these youths cannot love because they possess an unresponsive, cold-hearted nature, and he compares them to lovely flowers that lack fragrance. He also states that a youth with physical deformities is born that way as retribution for his unloving ways in a previous incarnation, and warns that handsome but unloving youths will suffer a similar fate.

But the youth questioning the master is not willing to place all of the blame on youths for being unresponsive in love, and suggests that sometimes a boy with the sincerest intentions will be misunderstood by an uncouth, insensitive man and will end up being accused of lacking love. The master dismisses this suggestion as highly unlikely. It is his opinion that such misunderstandings are relatively rare, and that reputations for cold-heartedness are usually deserved by the youths who acquire them.

The young questioner is not content to accept this, however, but responds by shifting the blame for cold-heartedness from youths onto adult men. The master objects to this strategy with a quote (actually, spurious) from Japan's greatest literary masterpiece, *The Tale of Genji*, to the effect that "love given to even the most ill-bred, insensitive man is not wasted," but the youth counters that *The Tale of Genji* is about heterosexual love (the love of women), not about homosexual love (the love of youths), and therefore the quote is inapplicable. The master disagrees vehemently: "If loving women is the only way of love, then how can 'the way of the youth' also be the way of love?" To prove his point, he lists past Chinese and Japanese examples of male love that illustrate the benefits of love between a man and a youth. He concludes that ancient precedent proves that it is proper for a youth to respond to a man's affections, for otherwise his youthful beauty is wasted. Part One concludes with a final injunction to samurai youths to be loving in their dealings with men:

> Evil does not cause evil only for others, neither does love benefit only others. It all circles back to become love directed at oneself. If a man tells you that he loves you, show your mastery of the rectitude of love and avoid error by returning his love, regardless of his status; thus should the heart [of a youth] be trained.

Part Two begins with a description of the flawed characters of some youths, based on seven types of "hearts" that they possess. There is the "merciless heart" of youths who reject a man's advances; the "vacillating heart" of youths who lead a man on but never commit themselves to love him; the "heart lacking Buddha-Nature" of youths who dare to criticize their male lover behind his back; the "heart of the Six Ways," belonging to youths who want to respond but are afraid of what others will say; the "greatly vacillating heart" of youths who make a vow of love with two men; the "thoughtless heart," belonging to youths who inform their lover of an interloper's identity, thus obliging him to engage in a duel to the death with the man; and the "heart calling at the gate," belonging to youths who become attached to a man but do not form a sexual relationship with him. The cure for all these character flaws, according to the master, is simple: "Youths ought to study 'the way' obediently and carefully."

The master then defines the stages of youth as a period of nine years from ages twelve to twenty, divided into three intervals of three years each. These intervals are compared to the three periods of time (*sansei*) codified in Buddhist metaphysics: past, present, and future. In the first stage, to age fifteen, the youth is still a child in need of instruction in "the way." This period is called the past. The next three years are called the present, when a youth's beauty is at its peak and he learns to love through proper training of his heart and mind. The final three years from age eighteen are called the future, when a youth matures and prepares for adulthood by further training himself in manly conduct. The master further develops the idea of karmic retribution for good and evil deeds, firmly placing the bond of man-youth love in the category of good deeds. Nevertheless, the meaning of the bond is primarily in the lesson of life's mutability that it teaches. The master concludes the catechism with a standard litany of Buddhist truth, that life is brief, that every meeting concludes in separation, that every gain leads to eventual loss. The book ends with a poem reiterating the theme that love and compassion alone have the power to redeem an otherwise unredeemably sorrowful existence.

4. Translation:
The Record of Heartfelt Friends (Shin'yûki, 1643)[3]

Part One.

I decided to pursue the way of the retired mountain hermit and spend my time reflecting on the world in which we live. First, it is obvious that the present life is an abode of dreams and illusions. In the course of our lives in this abode of dreams and illusions, the hearts of all people—highborn and lowborn alike—are beset by many unexpected sorrows and joys, and by order and chaos. How difficult it is to perceive the principle underlying this state of constant flux. Order and chaos in the heart originates from whether one's heart achieves intimacy with the hearts of others, or whether it fails to achieve such intimacy; thus, there is no other explanation but that all things proceed from the heart. Is that not what Tu Mu-zi meant when he wrote in *Ode of A-Fang Palace*, "The heart of one man is the heart of all men"?[4] Truly, is it not obvious that the source of grief and joy, order and chaos in one man's heart is the same for all men? In this regard, it seems to me that if we neglect the teachings of the sages and fail to emphasize compassion and love in our lives, we invite not only the destruction of our households but also certain death. Now, in China there were Chieh of the Hsia Dynasty and King Chou of the Shang Dynasty,[5] and in our country there was Governor Taira no Masatoki,[6] who knew nothing of the way of compassion and love: as a result, they lost their kingdoms and shortly thereafter even lost their lives.

Compassion and love alone ought to be practiced by all people throughout society, from the supreme ruler at the top to the common-folk below. Those who know nothing of compassion are in no way different from dogs and horses. [The five Confucian virtues of] brotherhood, righteousness, ceremony, wisdom, and trust are none other than [Buddhist] compassion and love. Again, it was the Buddha who taught that "He who has love will reach paradise, but the evil man will enter the cycle of rebirth." When you think of it, our bodies do not survive for long in this floating world. We resemble only withered blossoms before the wind, or ice in sunlight. Now, there are examples both in China and in our country, from ancient times to the present day, of poets and songsters who have written of life as "a floating world of dreams" and "a temporary shelter." There is even an old song that goes:

Even were I to live as long again
as I have lived till now,
brief it would be,
yes, how brief it would be.

This song is so true.

Nevertheless, though we may be enlightened to the brevity of our lives, we continue to mingle with the dust of this profane world, and thus it seems that our hearts are easily tempted into evil. This is because there are two diseases that afflict humankind. Evil has many manifestations, or so they say, but desire and lust is always its source. How can priest or layman, man or woman, rest undisturbed? First, to begin with no one can look at sexual beauty without being captivated by it. Now, then, if the feelings that arise are not satisfied, they torment the body in the form of a thousand griefs and a hundred diseases; some people are even driven to madness. Truly, the hearts of such people must be filled with pain, and therefore it is proper to respond warmly with love. Now, then, there are those who are incapable of love. And again, there are those who distinguish [whom to love] on the basis of status or wealth. Can this be called brotherhood? I have heard it said that "[A] gentleman makes no distinction on the basis of status or wealth," so, therefore, such youths will experience nothing good beyond the grave.

In general, there are numerous cases in both Japan and China of handsome youths incapable of love. In T'ang China there was a handsome youth named Yü-hsin whose beauty was without equal in the more than four-hundred provinces of T'ang China. Truly, it is said that "those who saw him extinguished their souls, and those who heard news of him bent their ears [for more]." Nevertheless, this youth knew nothing of the way of compassion and love. For this reason, a certain poet wrote *Ode Decrying Cold-heartedness* and placed it outside the youth's gate, blaming him for his lack of love. Yü-hsin did not heed the accusation, but continued anew each month and grew worse each day in his evil-hearted, mistaken way. As a result, due—no doubt—to the resentment of innumerable [men], he suddenly went mad in the spring of his sixteenth year and ended up wandering throughout the provinces and villages of the land, exposing himself to ridicule. He finally died in a place called Yang Zhou. Not one [of the men] felt the slightest regret at his death but, on the contrary, rejoiced. "They say that 'resentment can shatter boulders,' so its effect on the human body is only natural." Again, the story has been told for generations and is well known even today that Sô-fun, Lord of Yang Zhou, composed a poem on the occasion of passing Yü-hsin's grave:

The cold-hearted youth;
whether right or wrong,
I feel no sadness seeing Yû-hsin's grave.

In any case, [youths] ought to concentrate exclusively on cultivating compassion and love.

Again, in our own country—was it during the reign of Emperor Kôan?—there was a Lesser Captain of the Left named Noritoki, son of Hino Dainagon Hirotoki. His complexion was like that of a peach blossom awaiting spring, his body like a willow swaying languidly in the breeze, so beautiful that even Mao Shang and Hsi Tzu would have hidden their faces in shame. The emperor favored him above the rest, so his fellow courtiers "waited eagerly for the droppings of the well-fed horse."[7] Everything about Noritoki was so splendid that no man could resist falling in love, from courtiers and nobles all the way down to farmers. Among his admirers was a courtier named Sukéshigé, Middle Captain of the Palace, who with Noritoki was in attendance to the emperor. Sukéshigé once observed Noritoki up close in the guard's station at the Shishinden Palace, and from that moment he became lovesick and took to his bed. He pondered how [to contact Noritoki], but because he wanted to avoid discovery, he spoke of his feelings to no one. Nevertheless, it is the way of this floating world that feelings unavoidably make themselves known, and [soon] the entire capital was aware of the matter. Sukéshigé thought in his heart, "Well, since my name is the talk of the capital, my feelings must be as obvious as red maple leaves in autumn," and he made up his mind [to confess his love]. He composed a hundred songs in one night and sent them to Noritoki to plead his case, but Noritoki never responded. This was more than Sukéshigé could bear. He soon took to his sickbed, heartbroken, and eventually passed away. His angry spirit would not leave, however, and clung to Noritoki. Noritoki himself took ill and before long, in what was the third week after Sukéshigé's death, he also died.

Question: In any case, if we lack compassion and love, it is clear that there are many cases of retribution of this sort. Particularly in the present day, I have observed many youths, all of whom are equally handsome, like "a single branch of pear blossoms moistened in the spring rain, plum blossoms opening in the snow, or crab-apple blossoms that droop languorously." And yet, there are some youths who lack love. What are we to make of this?

Answer: It is for that reason the *Kokinshû* preface states: "A flower with little fragrance, such is a beauty who lacks love." The comparison may be fitting, but it does not go far enough. A handsome youth who lacks love is mean-spirited, the most undesirable trait in the world. Though there may be large numbers of youths in this floating world, handsome ones are rare and so [they ought to be loving]. Now then, there are those born with physical imperfections due to karma from past lives. These youths, as they reach their prime, will no doubt experience times of shame and moments of sorrow. The emotions generated by their suffering cannot be adequately compared to a mere mountain. As I see it, such youths once possessed great physical beauty in a previous life. As a result, they were desired by many men, but because their hearts were full of evil, the youths failed to comprehend the benefits of love. Finally, their lives came to and end and in the next life they suffered retribution for the seriousness of their sin and were made to endure the suffering of unlimited tortures. In the cycle of rebirth they happened to be reborn as human beings once again but, due to the above obstacle from a past life, were born physically imperfect. Clearly, this is retribution. It goes without saying that a youth so handsome that "a single smile elicits one hundred lusts" yet who lacks a loving heart is lost on the Way of Three Evils. Even if that were not so, is it not the case that he must suffer immediate shame?

Question: But for many youths, it may be a question of rank. What I mean is, imagine that a certain man falls in love with a youth. Then the youth, being exceptional in character, immediately establishes "a relationship of the ox's ear" with the man, and they sign oaths of love. Now then, the lover is also a man of exceptionally tender character, and together they are like Han Yun and Mao Liu. One day, the boy innocently asks, in the course of discussing the qualities of ten varieties of incense, "Please give me a cloth (*kin*) to place under the incense burner." His lover, being of low rank and uncouth, thinks he is referring to gold (*kin*) and later speaks ill of him. "Well now, how crude it is for a youth of his rank to express such greed for gold!" When others hear it, they naturally have no praise for him. He has suffered shame undeservedly. In this regard, I am reminded of Ku Yuan from the kingdom of So who drowned himself in a lake because he was wrongfully accused by his king, though he served his sovereign faithfully. When such uncouth men exist, no matter how much a youth desires to love a man, is he not destined to fail?

Answer: Such cases may exist, but do you suppose there are large numbers of youths in this world as splendid [as Ku Yuan]? Or do you suppose there are large numbers of youths deficient in love? I have given this matter careful thought, and in my experience youths as splendid [as Ku Yuan] are exceedingly rare.

Question: It may be the case that both sides are right, and both are wrong. Be that as it may, do you suppose there are large numbers of male lovers who know the intricacies of "the way of the youth"? Or do you suppose there are large numbers of male lovers who do not know them? In my experience, those who know the intricacies are rare.

Answer: Well, I think it is the Kashiwagi chapter of *The Tale of Genji* where it says that "the way of love defies logic." If you understand that concept, it is only natural that love be given to a man of even the most lowly and uncouth rank.

Question: Is *The Tale of Genji* about "the way of the youth"? I understood that it was Genji's character to love only women. In particular, I have never heard mention of "the way of the youth" in classical times.

Answer: If loving women is the only way of love, then how can "the way of the youth" be the way of love? And how can you say that "the way of the youth" is not talked about in ancient times? Even in olden times in T'ang China, Duke Zhuang of Chêng loved Tzu Tong, Duke Ling of Wei loved Mi-tzu Hsia,[8] King Ai of Wei loved Lord Long Yang,[9] Han [Emperor] Kao Tzu loved Chi Ju, Han Emperor Hui loved Hong Ju. Likewise, Emperor Wu loved Li Yen-nien, Emperor Ai loved Tong Hsian, Emperor Wen loved Teng T'ong,[10] and Tong P'o loved Chieh Sui.[11]

In our own land, also, in ancient times there was a courtier named Lord Tadashigé of Oku[12] who was the most powerful man in his day. Nevertheless, this man was arrogant and uncouth and knew nothing of the value of love. He despised good deeds and rejoiced over bad ones, practiced evil and avoided good, and was an unspeakably evil man. He had an only son by the name of Prince Shigémitsu. The boy was the opposite of his father in every way, from childhood possessed of a normal heart that rejoiced over good deeds and grieved over evil ones, full of compassion and deeply loving, and now at the age of fourteen he had become a handsome youth whose physical beauty was quite beyond compare. There was in the household a man named Kagémasa, who was remarkably attracted to Prince Shigémitsu's beauty, but due to his own low rank he feared to approach his young lord; try as he might to express his desire to meet, he could not bring himself to speak the words. Thinking that his unhappiness was obvious in the extreme and that his feelings would make themselves known, he merely suffered in silence. Prince Shigémitsu must have heard of the matter, for he immediately made an oath of love with Kagémasa; their love-making was "in heaven, two one-winged birds [flying side by side], on earth, two trees with grafted branches," and it goes without saying that the Prince loved him deeply. Nothing could compare with the gratitude in Kagémasa's heart.

A year passed quickly, and since it is the way of this floating world for people to despise the poor and the lowly, when the boy's father, Lord Tadashigé, found out about this matter, he thought "This is the work of that damned Kagémasa," and plotted to have him executed. Kagémasa had no idea of this, but when Prince Shigémitsu heard, he urgently summoned Kagémasa to him and explained the situation. "How I regret this development! Throughout the time of my oath of love with you, you have given me solid advice and loyal service, and your love for me was so great that you would gladly have given your life for me; as a result, I have felt happy and secure. Must I now remain behind in the world and spend my days in lonely sorrow? That you should be executed on my account is especially hard to bear," he said weeping bitterly, distraught that they must say farewell. Kagémasa heard him and said, "I am most grateful for your gracious words. It has been said that 'A samurai dies to prove his loyalty to his lord, but a son does not die to prove his filial piety.' I am but a low-ranking man in my prince's service, and have enjoyed your benevolence and love over and over again for more than a year; I can think of nothing I desire more than to be executed for your sake. If I cannot repay you in this life for the kind benevolence you showed me, it will surely be an obstacle to salvation in my next life, and my biggest failing in this one. If I die this very moment, I swear to repay your every kindness, even from the grave." He bowed deeply to Prince Shigémitsu and withdrew from his presence, and thereafter acted as if he knew nothing of the matter.

Many men appeared before Lord Tadashigé to receive their sentences of execution. Prince Shigémitsu could not bear it, and again summoned Kagémasa for an audience. "It seems that you will soon die. Since that is the case, put your life in my hands. Rather than die by the sword of another, let me be the one to slay you so that we may sit side by side on the same lotus leaf in the next world," he said, filled with grief, and as he spoke he sank to the floor. Kagémasa's heart was filled with gratitude; he put himself at the mercy of the Prince's sword and, at the age of twenty-five, received his death sentence. Shigémitsu immediately shaved his head and described his feelings in words that he wrote down in great detail and placed next to Kagémasa's corpse; he then set out in search of enlightenment. His parents, who remained behind, were consumed with regret and searched the provinces for their son, but Prince Shigémitsu was nowhere to be found. Overwhelmed by grief, both parents experienced enlightenment. Afterwards, Prince Shigémitsu spent three years engaged in various prayers for the repose of Kagémasa's soul and, at the age of seventeen, jumped to his death. All this occurred because both of his parents were arrogant and uncouth and had no comprehension of the brotherhood and righteousness of love, and thus they lost their only son in this manner. In actual fact, it is said that Monju Bosatsu[13] took human appearance in the form of Prince Shigémitsu. Lord Tadashigé's heart was unenlightened, so Monju took pity on him and, in order to undo his evil deeds and bring him to enlightenment, was born as his son and became the embodiment of the brotherhood and righteousness of love and jumped to his death; just as Monju had hoped, both husband and wife experienced enlightenment and ultimately became river pilots poling the boat of all-wisdom, experiencing true pleasure and escaping from the cycle of rebirth to be reborn in paradise.

The fact that such things occurred in ancient times proves that if a man takes a liking to you, you ought to respond with affection; only then will this floating world of ours function smoothly. It would be wise to ponder this point well. After all, in this floating world that is like a brief dream, here today and gone tomorrow, your peak of youthful beauty lasts but a moment, and you ought not waste even one moment of that beauty while it is yours. There is a poem in Chinese that expresses it this way:

Look closely, for youth speeds on;
Neither can long life be preserved in this world.
Beauty is not exempt from aging and decay;
So, love while your looks are fresh.

The period during which men will be attracted to you is but a brief one. Those of you who comprehend the value of love will enter "the special way" in this life, and by avoiding being thought ill of, even if you should die, you will without fail enter the way of truth.

This is exactly what the poem—by Zen master Ikkyû,[14] I think—means when it says,

Live your life
looking at the moon
and gazing at blossoms;
do not make it a Buddha, or waste it—
this body of yours.

If we ask what [Ikkyû] meant by writing thus, we see that it is a poem urging all people to train their hearts. "Looking at the moon" means that people with their clouded heart must look to the shining moon for clarity. "Blossoms" are a symbol of those things that you never tire of looking at and that others likewise never tire of looking at. "Gazing at" means that if someone takes a liking to you, on the basis of the benefits of love, you must give him your love and gaze into each other's eyes. "Live your life" means to live life in this uncertain world so as not to be spoken ill of or thought ill of by others. A regular youth of limited intelligence who trains his heart in this way and is well thought of by men in this life will surely enter the way of enlightenment in the next life. "Do not make it a Buddha" means that you must not die having lived your life with an uncommitted heart, being spoken ill of and thought ill of by others. "Or waste it—this body of yours" means that, though someone may have had the rare good-fortune of being born in human form, those in this life who are spoken ill of and thought ill of will surely enter the Path of Three Evils in the next life. This means, if someone fails to enjoy the pleasures of this life, what a waste his life will have been. The entire poem is a command to train yourself in the way of love. Whether highborn or lowborn, poor or rich, old or young, whether bird or beast, none can afford to despise love. And that is not all. An old poem states:

If you cause suffering,
there will always be retribution;
no one ever made an enemy
by being loving.

Evil does not cause evil only for others, neither does love benefit only others. It all circles back to become love directed at oneself. If a man tells you that he loves you, show your mastery of the rectitude of love and avoid error by returning his love, regardless of his status; thus should the heart be trained.

Part Two.

Question: All men, being by nature arrogant and uncouth, are ignorant of how to love; at such times, what ought they to do?
Answer: Love is like time: there are some who experience it with knowledge of its way, and others who experience it knowing nothing. To cultivate oneself enough to avoid violating the rules of proper conduct of this floating world does not require a complete grasp of the complexities of the way. Nevertheless, there are those who are completely ignorant of the rules of proper conduct. Among the things they do not know, first and foremost is the failure to distinguish between right and wrong: They use crude language or tell improper stories in front of youths. They lie. They keep silent when they ought to speak out and harbor evil in their hearts without cause. They fail to die when duty requires it and resent others for no reason. They stubbornly refuse to take advice; they alienate people with their pettiness and greed. They are intolerant of social obligations and accuse the innocent of wrong-doing. Though fools, they act as though they know it all. They are unreliable and lacking in cultivation. They forget the obligations they owe and treat their parents with disrespect. They have no compassion or love in their hearts. In general, there are many men of this sort. Their behavior cannot be called proper for a human being. Proper conduct for a human being would be the opposite of each of the items listed above; only then could it be called manly conduct.

To cultivate oneself so as to avoid violating the rules of proper conduct, a youth need not have a complete grasp of the way. Youths need only be obedient in upholding its precepts. For the man in love, depending on the feelings of the youth, his love may turn to joy or it may turn to resentment; thus, some youths distinguish on the basis of high or low rank and use restrained or unrestrained words accordingly. Such actions are caused by what is called a "Merciless Heart," and are a great disgrace. Only by making no distinction between highborn and lowborn and always, in all matters, properly distinguishing right from wrong can love be called a "way". Sometimes there are youths who, though very handsome, lack a lover. Seeing such a boy, there are occasionally men who fall so deeply in love they are willing to die, but though their feelings are clearly discernable in their eyes, they go on day after day unable to tell the boy how they feel. There a youths who, even when they realize how the man feels, not only refuse to love him, but will criticize the man who loves them. This, too, results from the "Merciless Heart."

Again, there are occasionally youths without lovers who will insist that they have a lover every time they respond to a man's expressions of interest, but when asked for proof they can never provide it. Such an action is caused by what is called a "Vacillating Heart," which is a particularly vulgar condition.

Each of the above problems is the topic of widespread discussion, but there are youths who take no notice whatsoever. No youth, even one who is happy without a lover, should refuse a man who expresses a sincere interest in him. The reason they refuse a man who loves them is because they take his feelings lightly. This man's feelings are the result of karma from a previous life, and once he falls in love his suffering is without respite night and day. No matter how painful the suffering, however, he never thinks ill of the youth. Because he never thinks ill of him, the man considers giving his life for him, and even when gazing at the moon or cherry blossoms, his heart feels no pleasure; it is full of thoughts of the youth. The unbearable suffering he endures cannot be adequately compared to a mountain. Is it possible to justify rejecting a man who is suffering in this way? In general, the human heart can be discerned in a single glance. In particular, the man whose interest is sincere can easily be discerned. Even if the man is an enemy of a youth's father, if the youth judges him to be a man who sincerely loves him, the youth should tell himself that the man picked him out of all the youths in the world because of a karmic bond from a previous life, and be grateful for his loving attention; he should not take the man's feelings lightly, but in all things do everything in his power to please him. If he does so, the man will gladly (as the proverb says) "for a single day of your love, give up one hundred years of life," and the man's happiness will be greater than a mountain. Thereby, he will desire further intimacy. At that time, if the youth somehow finds a way to give himself to the man in a vow of love, so they cultivate their feelings for each other and share three years of intimacy by his side, is it not like a dream within a dream? Not only that, but his good name will live through the ages; but the world being unstable and life brief, it seems that some still think they disgrace themselves if they love a man. There is no misconception as hard to dislodge as this one.

Again, there are occasionally youths with a lover whom they act like they love, but in their hearts they revile him. Such youths possess what is called a "Heart Lacking Buddha-Nature," and are evaluated at the same level as dumb beasts. The reason for this is, once a youth binds himself to a man as his lover, their relationship ought to pattern itself after the relationship between parent and child. That is why, when a boy refers to his lover, he touches his thumb ("parent finger") to his little finger ("child finger"). With a bond as close as that of parent and child, if a child makes light of his parent, can such a youth be called human?

Again, there are youths whose hearts are gentle, but fearing what people might say, they are unable to respond with love. They possess what is called the "Heart of the Six Ways."[15]

Again, sometimes a man will fall in love with a youth who already has a lover, and it reaches the point where they actually meet. When the man cuts his thighs and wrists and vows to kill himself [if the youth refuses him], some youths immediately give their consent. They possess what is called the "Greatly Vacillating Heart". Above all else, it is the single most important precept of "the different way" that once a youth makes a contract with a man, he ought never speak the same vow with another man, even in jest or in his dreams—even for a moment, even if it is a lie, even if the other man actually kills himself.

Sometimes, when a youth who has a lover receives a love letter from another man, he does not consider what is right and wrong, and tells his lover about it. He has what is called a "Thoughtless Heart," which is a tragic waste. No man can idly sit by if he hears that an interloper wants to force himself on the boy he loves. If the lover is kept unaware it need not lead to a confrontation, but being a mere youth, if the youth thoughtlessly tells his lover, it immediately becomes a contest of egos between the lover and the interloper; inevitably in such cases, someone ends up being killed for no reason. Again, a lover ought to constantly train himself to notice such situations without having to be told by someone else. And again, a youth ought to speak freely to his lover regarding questions of proper conduct. It is a mistake, however, to tell the lover something without first considering what is right and wrong.

Even if a youth is approached by a man who is uncouth, he ought not reveal a hint of it to his lover, but should refuse him on the basis of what is right and wrong in love, and if the man is truly, truly ignorant of right and wrong, and threatens to end his life, then the youth ought to write down his thoughts in a final testament and die without regrets. This is what Confucius meant when he said, "It is possible to ask the way in the morning, and be dead by nightfall." The youth's lover who is left behind will be shocked when he hears the news and, gazing at the words in the boy's final testament, will experience true enlightenment and pray for the repose of the youth's soul for the number of days equivalent to the length of their relationship. And when he reaches the final day of his prayers, in most cases he jumps to his death.

Again, there are times when a youth shares a deep intimacy with a man, but he does not enter the "way of the youth" and the relationship is aborted. This is called "The Heart Calling at the Gate," and deserves punishment as severe as if the youth had incurred the wrath of his father. Taking the preceding points into consideration, youths ought to study "the way" obediently and carefully.

Now, "the way of the youth" lasts for an interval of nine years, from ages twelve to age twenty. That interval is divided into three parts of three years each, which can be likened to the three periods of time: past, present, and future.

The first three years, beginning with age twelve, are the past. During this period the youth is still quite a child, so *shudô* "the way of the youth" is written with the characters *shu* "primary", *dô* "child", and *dô* "way".

The next three years, beginning with age fifteen, can be likened to the present. This is the middle of the nine years of "the way of the youth", when a youth is at his peak. He develops deep respect for the rights and wrongs of love, strives not to go against the way's precepts, and trains himself to apply what he has learned to every aspect of life; unsurpassed in his heart and speech, he is at his peak in this period. For this reason, the word for these three years is written with the characters *koto naru* "being special" and *michi* "way" and is pronounced *shudô*. The meaning of the word "being special" is that the youth is outstanding in both heart and speech.

The next three years from age eighteen can be likened to the future. This is, namely, the interval when "the way of the youth" comes to a conclusion, so training in manly conduct is now added to earlier training in the heart of "the special way", and without wasting a single moment of the precious time remaining to him, the youth must become enlightened in all matters. The reason twenty years customarily represents one generation in human life, and why "the way of the youth" ending in twenty years is referred to as one generation, is all because of this fact. Therefore, the word for these three years is written with the characters for *owaru* "ending" and *michi* "way" and is pronounced *shudô*. In this way, once a youth reaches his twentieth year is it not the case that he will never again possess in this life "the beautiful complexion and figure of a blossom"?

Since the years fly by thus in a moment, for a youth not to love while his beauty is fresh could hardly be appropriate, could it? Some youths may have been born predestined to have only the twenty years mentioned above as their allotted span of life. If such a youth shows no compassion or love and dies at an early age, what will become of him in the world to come? Do not the feelings of tenderness that move a youth to love [a man] remain with him as good deeds after his death? The way this works is, if a youth gives even a little love in his early years, the recipient will remember it for the rest of his life, and likewise others will not forget the debt of gratitude for the love the youth gave long ago, so that never for a moment will he be thought ill of, allowing him to achieve True Buddhahood for his good deeds. But those who show no love in their youth, though they reach adulthood, will plot only evil in their hearts from dawn to dusk. Occasionally, they may put on a show of decency in front of others, but in private they curse and revile blameless men and envy their good deeds. Such people will earn the enmity of everyone they meet, and should they die, the news would be met with rejoicing. Retribution for the grave sin of earning the resentment of others lingers for three cycles of suffering and rebirth.

The Buddha himself taught:

If for many years
a man holds evil in his heart,
and puts on a show of good while cursing the Buddha,
he earns a boundless burden of sin.[16]

This means that there are both good and evil men living in this world. The hearts of evil men are always resentful of others, but when they meet someone they put on a friendly expression and deceive them with flattering words, while behind their backs they curse and revile good men innocent of any wrongdoing. Such people must bear the burden of a sin too heavy to weigh. Living things, whether human or non-human, are ultimately not divided into good and evil. It is one body that produces good thoughts, and one body that produces evil thoughts, so when we reach the point where we can simply dispense with evil thoughts and train ourselves to have only good thoughts, there we find no division between good and evil. That is why the sutras teach that "The three cycles of suffering and rebirth are based on the heart alone; there is no law outside the law governing the heart."

The heart that gives love is good, and the heart that receives love is also good. But a person who lives twenty years will eventually be beset with the eight sufferings, and he will find that his burden of sin easily grows heavier and becomes harder to relieve. At such a time, our only hope is to become enlightened to the good heart in this temporary dwelling place and to pray for rebirth in paradise. In particular, it is said that "human life is like dew on a morning-glory, here in the morning and gone by nightfall." Moreover, it is clear that life is unpredictable for old and young alike. There is nothing as fleeting as the dwelling place that is this world. For that reason, Li P'o has written:

Heaven and earth is a journey home for all things.
Time is a traveler for a hundred generations.
This floating world is like a dream;
How often is pleasure ours to give?

Nevertheless, no one knows what karma he brings from former lives. Perhaps he embraced greed, lived for money, suffered physical pain, and committed serious crimes. People, plants, birds, and beasts all receive, each and every, a life of pleasure or pain determined by karma from past lives. Human beings, however, possess the same body of Buddha nature and are without a doubt capable of achieving Buddhahood in through enlightenment in this world. As for the obvious good and evil we see in this world, the good is good from previous lives and the evil is evil from previous lives. Both good and evil are retribution from lives that came before. By observing the present, we can know the future.

In any case, the three cycles of rebirth are filled with suffering. There is no pleasure for any living thing. Our lives in this temporary dwelling place, all phenomena are like a dream. A career is short-lived, and glory comes to an end. We flourish for an hour, and live but an instant. A wife and child become unwelcome bonds, and attachments burden the heart. Lust is the source of suffering, and ambition leads to grief. Where there is life, there is also death. Where there is pleasure, there is also pain. A man in his prime cannot escape decline; those we meet are destined to leave. The body is like a flame before the wind, and life is like dew on the grass. Fleeting is this world, and unreliable are our bodies. "There is no rest in the three worlds of rebirth, like a burning house in which we are trapped." It is exactly as the Buddha teaches. The whole of the law returns to one point:

The body, the heart.
If we leave behind
The darkness of the heart,
There, is compassion and love.
The moon at daybreak.

Kan'ei 20 [1643], Eighth Month, an Auspicious Day.

---

[1] *Shin'yûki* is discussed in English briefly in Watanabe Tsuneo and Iwata Jun'ichi, *The Love of the Samurai: A Thousand Years of Japanese Homosexuality* (London: Gay Men's Press, 1989), pp. 110-111, where the title is translated "Book for the friends of the soul"; and in Ihara Saikaku, *The Great Mirror of Male Love* (Stanford: Stanford University Press, 1990), pp. 6-7.

[2] Noma Kôshin, ed. *Kinsei shikidô ron, Nihon shisô taikei* (Tokyo: Iwanami Shoten, 1976), pp. 60 and 379.

[3] Translation based on the annotated, modern print version of the text in Noma, pp. 7-25. Paragraph breaks follow Noma.

[4] Ode written upon viewing the burned ruins of the imperial palace, built by the First Emperor of Chin.

[5] The names Chieh and Chou, last rulers of the Hsia and Shang Dynasties respectively, are used as a synonym for tyranny. From *Shi chi*.

[6] Unknown. Possibly a mistaken reference to the regent Taira no Kiyomori, whose political demise and death is the subject of the 13th century *Tale of the Heike* (*Heike monogatari*).

[7] An expression indicating others flattered the emperor's favorite in an effort to benefit themselves.

[8] Duke Ling of Wei (534-493 B.C.); the relationship is recorded in *Han Fei tzu*. See Bret Hinsch, *Passions of the Cut Sleeve* (Berkeley: University of California Press, 1990), pp. 20-22.

[9] Hinsch, pp. 32-33.

[10] Hinsch, pp. 35-37.

[11] The poet Su Shih (1036-1101), also known as Su Tong P'o, describes his love of Li Chieh Sui in a poem called "The Wind and Water Cave."

[12] Michinoku, the northernmost provinces of Japan making up modern Tôhoku.

[13] *Monju shiri*, was a virtual patron saint of youths loved by men, due to a pun on the name, *shiri* also meaning "ass." Sanskrit: *Mañjú srî bodhisattva*, diety of wisdom.

[14] Ikkyû Sôjun (1394-1481), a brilliant and eccentric priest, said to have been the illegitimate son of Emperor Go-Komatsu (r. 1392-1412).

[15] Among the Six Ways of Hell is the way of the hungry ghost, a form of torture in which starving spirits are repeatedly tempted by food, but when they try to eat, the food bursts into flame and is consumed by fire. The analogy is with youths who desire to partake of love with a man but are prevented by scruples.

[16] From the *Lotus Sutra*.

VI. Giovanni Vitiello

Taoist Themes in Chinese Homoerotic Tales

The study of any issues related to sex in the Chinese cultural context cannot ignore the Taoist theories on sex, and in particular their speculations on the relation between sex and immortality.

Unlike many Christian traditions, where sex has always been viewed as a temptation, a major obstacle in the path towards God, in ancient Taoism sexual practices were seen as a special field of self-cultivation. Ancient Taoist practices and rituals involving sex were considered part of the training of the adept in his attempt to gain immortality. Taoist cosmology and physiology are based upon the belief that every form of life is the result of the interaction between two forces, *yin* (female, passive, dark, etc.) and *yang* (male, active bright, etc.). It follows that men and women incorporate both elements. Taoists believed that the sexual meeting with a woman through the contact with her *yin* potential allowed the male adept to reinforce his *jing* ("seminal essence") with a consequent benefit for his *qi* ("breath," or "vital principle"). Taoist physiology identifies the *qi* with the principle of life, and therefore also with that of eternal life. The semen, *jing*, is a male's most precious property, and for this reason it has to be carefully guarded and properly enriched.[1]

The reverse was also contemplated, and some texts therefore warn the adept to abstain from sexual contact with women who, knowing sexual techniques, could use the exchange of essences to their advantage. This fear has given birth to a whole literature on sexual vampirism, usually involving demons who disguise themselves as beautiful women and who seduce young men, and, thereby, sap them of their *yang* potential.

If sex, therefore, is a means to perfection, one wonders whether the use of such practices is invariant with regard to the gender identity of the partners. The basic sources used by Maspero and Van Gulik—the first scholars to explore the topic of sexology in connection with Taoism—are the few extant sex manuals. But since these manuals were meant to be used by heterosexual couples, they do not talk about homosexuality at all. Speculating on the Taoist perspective on male homosexuality, Van Gulik sums up his evidence by saying:

> Literary sources in general adopt a neutral attitude as long as it [i.e. male homosexuality] is engaged in by two grown-up persons, it being taken that intimate contact between two *yang* elements can not result in a total loss of the vital force for either of them.[2]

One can expand this by saying that in a religion in which physical and spiritual immortality coincide, and the concepts of sin and sickness are strongly related, sexual hygiene is at the same time an ethico-religious and a medico-physiological issue. It follows that a certain sexual practice that is considered dangerous from a medical point of view will also carry a moral sanction. Vice-versa, if there is no moral disapproval of it, it is likely that, also from the point of view of the sexual theories, that practice would be regarded as harmless at the very least.

This hypothesis seems to be confirmed by the fact that, when the author of the sixteenth century *materia medica Bencao gangmu* (General Inventory of Pharmaceutics), Li Shizhen (1518-1593), talks about *feinan* ("non-male") and *feinü* ("non-female"), he always refers to a deficiency in reproductive function, and never to anomalies in sexual behavior.[3] There seems to be no idea of homosexuality as a sexual perversion, or as sickness in Chinese traditional medicine. Moreover, to my knowledge, homosexuality never appears in the Taoist scriptures as an object of interdiction. The main issue, in medicine as well as in morality, is elsewhere. A homosexual liaison can be as dangerous as a heterosexual one in that it may cause, through an excessive activity, a dispersion of the vital spirit. The loss of *qi* from a merely pathological standpoint is the origin of sickness and eventually the cause of death, while, in general, from the religious point of view it represents an obstacle to the attainment of immortality.

One can quite safely say that since in traditional China male homosexuality is just one option of male sexuality, the medical as well as the moral criteria according to which it is judged are basically the same as those for male heterosexuality.[4] This is probably why references to the Taoist position on male homosexuality in the technical literature (in the *Taoist Canon,* for instance) are scarce, making the study of the topic difficult to pursue. Yet, literary sources, in particular fiction, often provide traces that allow us to speculate. Without referring to primary religious sources, I shall discuss a few tales in which homoeroticism is connected with Taoist themes. These may very well reflect, although indirectly, the vision of Taoists on sex between males.

Most of the stories that I will talk about come from an anthology called *Duanxiu pian* (The Cut Sleeve)[5] compiled sometime during the last century by a man of whom we know only the pseudonym: Ameng of Wu. His work was based on a previous anthology included in *Qing shi* (History of Love), a collection attributed to Feng Menglong (1574-1646). The stories I will examine date roughly from the seventeenth to the eighteenth centuries.

"The Carpenter's Son"[6]

A Taoist priest falls in love with the young son of a carpenter, and one day, using some charms, hypnotizes him and brings him to his house to seduce him. He is on the verge of satisfying his desire twice, but both times he refrains at the last moment. Here is the description of the first wave of remorse:

> The priest pulled him towards the bed; he caressed and hugged him, blandishing him with seductive words. He had just stripped and come up close to him, when, vexed, he suddenly withdrew, and sitting up said, "Have I cultivated the Tao for more than two hundred years to be defeated by this beautiful boy?"
> For a long time he reflected on it. Again he lay down next to the boy, watching and caressing his whole body, and with regret said, "But such a beautiful boy would be difficult to meet even in one thousand years." Even if I indulge in lust, thus violating my Tao, yet, if for two hundred years I exercise my vital spirit, what is the use of remorse?"[7]

Finally, the priest, to extinguish his desire, resorts to stabbing himself in the arm. For this reason he is praised at the end by the commentator. It is clear that this story does not involve a moral condemnation of homosexuality. There is in fact no reason to believe that the Taoist hesitates due to the fear of committing a sinful act, where the sin arises from the homosexual nature of the union. In this case the sin that is, the danger to health, is in having sex as such. The homosexual nature of the relation is very likely irrelevant, since the fact that the sexual union is between two males does not affect the validity of the general rule expressed in the sex manuals that loss of semen affects the project of self-cultivation. The Taoist's behavior exemplifies the principle of "internal alchemy" (*neidan*), according to which the disciple of the Tao should, so to speak, make love inside himself, with his own *yin* and his own *yang*, without needing a partner at all.[8]

Stories About Old Men

"The Two Old Men"[9] tells first the story of a young man who sodomizes an old man, and then, as a sort of explanation, a second story about two old men who are lovers. In the conclusion the commentator expresses his surprise at the two accounts and reflects on the meaning of those sexual affairs. He mentions a theory attributed to a certain Immortal Ma Xiutou who stated:

> There is in them [i.e. boys] a real *yin* essence which can be grasped. It belongs to the revitalizing techniques: one can have sex not only with women, but also with men.[10]

The commentator seems to be ready to accept the theory (though confining it to the realm of popular magical cults, believing that it cannot belong to orthodox Taoism); his objection is: "But in grasping the essence of an old man, what advantage can there be?"

Similarly, the story "The Old Gardener,"[11] about an old man having a homosexual affair with a male ghost who used to be his wife in a previous life (but by someone believed to be a fox-spirit), concludes with the following comment:

> Someone says, "It was a fox that wanted to seduce the old man, that's why he made all that story up. But, in fact, when foxes seduce, they do it because they are attracted by beauty and in order to absorb the vital spirit. But, a chicken skin or a crane hair, what beauty do they have to enjoy, what vital spirit to suck?"[12]

The tone of the commentator is basically the same in both instances. Surprise at something that is hardly understandable, an eccentricity on the border of enigma. By contrast, it is indirectly suggested that, if the older man had sodomized the young man, or the young man sodomized another young man, or the fox-spirit had selected a young victim instead of an old one, in all such cases homosexual relations would be considered normal, in the sense of rational (although, in the case of the fox-spirit, in a vampiristic logic). The cause of the commentator's surprise is the age of the partners. The stress is on the fact that a sexual union with an old man cannot be functional or nourishing in the process of augmentation of *qi*, given the weakness of their *jing*. A sexual relation between two old men who have, as hinted at by the commentator in the first of the two stories "retired deep into the mountain to cultivate the Tao," does not make any sense because sex with an old man cannot cause any physiological improvement in effecting the transformation of a human being into an immortal.

The surprise at the young man's raping of the old man is also socially motivated, given the unusual distribution of roles. A young man is more likely to play a sexually passive role, the opposite of what happens in this story. Old men playing an active role would not generate surprise unless it involved an excessive sexual activity, as shown by the story entitled "Zhang Youwen,"[13] in which an old man, asked by a friend about the secret to his good health, given that he has numerous young male lovers, answers with the following joke:

> On this matter my Tao is this: to use the *Sūtra of the Heart* (Xin jing) a lot, and the *Sūtra of Testicles* only a little. That's why I don't get any sickness.[14]

Behind the friend's question there is obviously the belief that sexual activity in old age should be reduced. Behind the old man's answer is the confirmation of that belief, together with the suggestion that aesthetic appreciation of a young beauty can partially replace sexual activity while benefitting health. It is important to keep in mind that these ideas refer to sexuality in general, although they happen to be expressed here in a homoerotic context.

The position attributed to the Immortal Ma Xiutou reflects the vampiristic motif that seems to underlie much of Taoist theories on the nourishment of the *qi*. The concept of the young man as a source of nourishing energies expands the theory of the sex manuals on the benefits of sleeping with young women. The perspective is unchanged: on one side we have the Taoist, the cultivator of immortality, and on the other side the sources of energy—now a woman, now a boy, now the moon-rays, now cinnabar. Ma Xiutou is not praising male homosexuality *per se,* but rather young men as an optional source of energies for self-cultivation in the process of gaining immortality. This affirmation refers to boys (*tong*), even if in his conclusive formula he talks about "sex with women" and "sex with men," without making distinctions on the basis of age.

Stories About Supernatural Beings

Some stories involve homosexual relation between human beings and demons or gods. When demons (often fox-spirits) are involved, the sexual pattern behind the story is always the same. A devilish creature in disguise (sometimes a woman, sometimes a young man, sometimes an invisible being) seduces a young man who eventually gets sick and dies unless positive magical powers come to his aid. What is described is a sexual vampiristic experience, the exploitation of someone's energies by a succubus. An example in *The Cut Sleeve* is "The Young Shepherd," the story of a boy raped by a fox spirit which is finally persuaded to abandon its victim.[15] The homoerotic tales of *The Cut Sleeve* on this topic represent a variation on the vast Chinese literary theme of sexual vampirism.

The stories entitled "The Graduate Lü Zijing"[16] and "The Quans' Son and the Zhangs' Son"[17] involve the divinity Wulang (or Wutong), known for his lust for young women.[18] His strongly sexual characterization explains his versatile desire.

"Lü Zijing" ties the story of a young scholar who looses his mind after the death of his lover. Later, thanks to the help of a ghost who sympathizes with his feelings and to the magical powers of a Taoist priest, he finds out that his beloved has been kidnapped by the god Wutong. He manages to reunite with him for eternity by joining the world of the ghosts.

The story "The Quans' Son and the Zhangs' Son" is divided into two episodes. In the first one Wulang takes away a young man from a family of Suzhou merchants by employing him as his assistant (and consequently causing him to die). In the second episode the death of a young man, also a victim of Wulang, is avoided thanks to the talismans and the incantations of a magician.

These last two stories do not stress the aspect of sexual vampirism by demons. Wulang here seems to be more drawn to certain men because of a selective romantic attraction than a blind vampiristic compulsion. Yet, it remains clear that the kidnapping by a demon, even by a demon in love, leads to a fatal destiny, the same way contact with a succubus does.

What would happen if a human had a sexual relation with an Immortal instead of a demon? Could it be nourishing for the man's *qi* ? Given, in fact, that sex is a vehicle for the transmission of vital energy, it should follow that, from the point of view of an adept, for instance, sexual union with a Taoist master or with an Immortal should be regarded as augmenting the vital spirit, and therefore profitable.

"A False Immortal Creates Great Confusion at the Temple of Huaguang"

Such an hypothesis seems to underlie the behavior of the protagonist of a story included in Feng Menglong's *Jingshi tongyan* (Common Words to Warn the World). "A False Immortal Creates Great Confusion at the Temple of Huaguang"[19] tells of a beautiful young scholar named Wei, who is visited one night by a man who claims to be the Immortal Lü Dongbin,[20] who has come to help the young scholar to transform himself into a supernatural creature. The boy is very flattered and grateful, and invites his benefactor to stay for the night. Once in bed, the supposed god asks the young Wei to unclothe himself so that his own energy can influence him more effectively. To eliminate any trace of doubt in the young man's mind, Lü tells him the story of the Han general Huo Qubing (140-117 B.C.), who had fallen ill after having refused the sexual advances of a god. The latter, beseeched then by Huo's friends to save his life, says that he knew of Huo Qubing's physical weakness, and that he had come to offer him a chance of being nourished by his own "extreme *yin (taiyin).* The general had not understood the good intentions of the god, and so had died.

Convinced by the story the 'Immortal' has told him, Wei becomes his lover. Their relation turns into a *ménage à trois* when the 'Immortal' one night brings along a beautiful lady whom he introduces as the female-Immortal He Xiangu.[21] She is also said to be able to give him "extreme *yin.*" The three of them engage in a long secret relationship, and the young scholar becomes more and more seriously ill. His father asks then for the help of a Taoist master, who is defeated by the apparently superior devilish power. Meanwhile, in his delirium, Wei reveals the whole story of the nocturnal visits. Wei's father and friends proceed to make a sacrifice at the Temple of the Bodhisattva Huaguang. The Bodhisattva informs them that the two 'Immortals' were in fact male and female turtle-spirits. The gods, moved, have already sought them out and beheaded them. The Bodhisattva recommends that Wei's father make a soup with the turtle-spirits' shells buried under a certain tree, and have the young man drink it. So it happens and quickly the young Wei regains his vital essence and therefore his health.

I conclude from this that (a) the homosexual theme is secondary, the stress being rather on the devilish vampirism and the related problem of loss-augmentation of vital spirit; (b) in theory, in a homosexual union, a profitable exchange of vital potency can take place, as shown by the discourse of the false immortal Lü and by the consequent behavior of the young man, who clearly is lured by the illusion of transfusing divine essence into his own body.

The validity of such an hypothesis is further supported by the mythological account—in a heterosexual frame—about the attainment of Immortality by He Xiangu herself, which took place when the Immortal Lü Dongbin released his semen during sexual intercourse with her.[22] In conclusion, it is justified to say that homoerotic discourse in Taoism, as reflected in these sources, does not involve moral or medical condemnation. Homosexuality poses an enigma only when it involves old men as passive partners or when sexual excess (homosexual as well as heterosexual) does not lead to a deterioration of health. As for sexual contacts with supernatural beings, if they are demons, they cause loss of *qi* and eventual death; if they are Immortals, they may on the contrary be profitable on the path to Immortality.

---

[1] These ideas are also at the basis of that complex of practice that go under the name of *huanjing bunao* ("to guide the semen back to replenish the brain"). On this topic cf., Henri Maspero, "Methods of 'Nourishing the Vital Principle' in the Ancient Taoist Religion," in his *Taoism and Chinese Religion* (Amherst, MA, University of Massachussets Press, 1981), pp. 445-554. In general, on Chinese sexuality see Robert van Gulik, *Sexual Life in Ancient China: A Preliminary Survey of Chinese Sex and Society from ca. 1500 B.C. till 1644 A.D.* (Leiden, Holland: E.F. Brill, 1961), 392 pgs.

[2] Van Gulik, p. 48.

[3] Cf., Charlotte Furth, "Androgenous Males and Deficient Females: Biology and Gender in Sixteenth and Seventeenth-Century China," *Late Imperial China* 9.2 (December 1988), pp. 1-31. In particular see pp. 4-5.

[4] Cf. my Master's Thesis, *"The Peasant Who Was Raped by a Dragon" and Other Stories: Ming and Qing Homoerotic Tales from* **The Cut Sleeve** (University of California at Berkeley, Berkeley, Spring 1990).

[5] The text of the *Duanxiu pian* (hereafter DXP) can be found in *Xiangyan congshu* (The Collection of the Fragrant Beauty), 9.2, pp. 1a-22a. The only translation of the text is the one I have done in Italian: *Ameng di Wu, La Manica Tagliata,* a cura di G. Vitiello (Palermo, Italy: Sellerio, 1990), 142 pgs.

[6] DXP, pp. 18b-19a.

[7] DXP, p. 19a.

[8] Cf., Kristopher M. Schipper, "Science, Magic and the Mystique of the Body," in Michel Beurdeley (ed.), *The Clouds and the Rain: The Art of Love in China* (Rutland, VT, and Tokyo, Japan: C.E. Tuttle Co., 1969), pp. 14-20.

[9] DXP, pp. 19b-20a.

[10] DXP, p. 20a.

[11] DXP, pp. 18a-b.

[12] DXP, p. 18b.

[13] DXP, pp. 14a.-15a.

[14] DXP, p. 14b. The *Sutra of the Heart* is the *Prajnaparamita sutra.*

[15] DXP, pp. 16a-b.

[16] DXP, pp. 15b-16a.

[17] DXP, p. 15a.

[18] Sometimes the name indicates a team of five gods. Cf., Wolfram Eberhard, *The Local Cultures of South and East China* (Leiden, NL: E.F. Brill, 1968), pp. 61-63.

[19] *Jingshi tongyan*, ch. 27.

[20] One of the Eight Immortals.

[21] The only woman among the Eight Immortals.

[22] Cf., Kristopher M. Schipper, *Le corps taoïste* (Paris, France: Fayard, 1982), pp. 212-213. A similar account is also given about the goddess Xi Wangmu (cf., Maspero, p. 530).

VII. Notes on Contributors

José Ignacio Cabezón, Ph.D., is an assistant professor of the philosophy of religion at Iliff School of Theology, Denver, CO. He is a member of the Steering Committee of the Gay Men's Issues in Religion Group of the American Academy of Religion. Among his numerous publications is the article "Vasubandhu's **Vyakhyayukti** on the Authenticity of the Mahayana Sutras," which is published in a collection of essays, *Traditional Hermeneutics in South Asia*, ed. by J. Timm (Albany: SUNY Press, 1991).

J. Michael Clark, Ph.D., is currently co-chair of the Gay Men's Issues in Religion Group of the American Academy of Religion and is both an "independent scholar" & a part-time instructor in the Freshman English Program of Georgia State University (Atlanta). Among his numerous publications are *A Place to Start: Toward an Unapologetic Gay Liberation Theology* (Dallas, TX: Monument Press, 1989); & *Theologizing Gay: Fragments of Liberation Activity* (Oak Cliff, TX: Minuteman Press, 1991).

Gary David Comstock, Ph.D., is the University Protestant Chaplain and visiting assistant professor of religion at Wesleyan University. His work, *Violence Against Lesbians and Gay Men*, was published by Columbia University Press in 1991.

Jeffrey J. Kripal earned his B.A. at Conception Seminary College before coming to the University of Chicago Divinity School, where he is now a Ph.D. candidate in the History of Religions Program. He is researching and writing a dissertation on the relationship between eroticism and mystical experience, entitled "Kālī's Child: The Mystical and the Erotic in Mahendranath Gupta's *Śrīśrīrāmakṛṣṇakathāmṛta*." He and his wife, Julie, live with their daughter, Jenna, in Chicago.

Paul Gordon Schalow, Ph.D., is a scholar of Japanese literature. He is an associate professor in the Department of East Asian Languages and Cultures at Rutgers University, N.J. He has published a translation the *The Great Mirror of Male Love* by Ihara Saikaku (Stanford, CA: Stanford University Press, 1990). Presently he is working on a study of the construction of male love in 17th century Japanese vernacular literature.

Michael L. Stemmeler, Ph.D., is currently co-chair of the Gay Men's Issues in Religion Group of the American Academy of Religion and an assistant professor of religion at Central Michigan University. As leading co-editor of this series, he is the author of *Gays--A Threat to Society? Social Policy in Nazi Germany and the Aftermath*, in *Homophobia & the Judaeo-Christian Tradition* (series volume 1; Dallas, TX: Monument Press, 1990), pp. 69-93. He has co-produced a video on the experience of gay life and homophobia on the college campus, *In Our Own Words: Lesbian, Gay and Bisexual Students at CMU* (Mt. Pleasant, MI: CMU-A/V Productions, 1992). He is the author of several papers on medical ethics and AIDS, and is currently working in the areas of gay spiritual identity formation and the values of non-traditional relationships.

Giovanni Vitiello, M.A. Born in Naples, Italy, in 1962. Graduate of the University of Rome (1985). Thanks to two fellowships offered by the Government of the People's Republic of China within the Cultural Exchange Program with the Italian Government, he spent two years at the Beijing University (1984-1986). As a recipient of a Fullbright fellowship he later came to the University of California at Berkeley to continue his Ph.D. studies at the Department of East Asian Languages. The topic of his dissertation is homoeroticism in the Chinese literature of the Ming and the Qing.